HOW TO [illegible]... EXAM...AND REMAKE THE WORLD

LAST WILL AND TESTAMENT

I leave to the students of this world all the "As" they desire and as a good a life as they're willing to fight for, along with the little bit of wisdom I've acquired on how to get both.

HOW TO TAKE AN EXAM...AND REMAKE THE WORLD

BERTELL OLLMAN

Montréal/New York/London

Black Rose Books No. DD293
Hardcover ISBN: 1-55164-171-2 (bound)
Paperback ISBN: 1-55164-170-4 (pbk.)

Canadian Cataloguing in Publication Data
Ollman, Bertell, 1935-
How to take an exam...and remake the world

Includes bibliographical references.
Hardcover ISBN: 1-55164-171-2 (bound)
Paperback ISBN: 1-55164-170-4 (pbk.)

1. Politics. 2. Education, Higher-Humour. 3. Education, Higher. 4. Examinations--Handbooks, Manuals, etc. I. Title.

LC191.0442 2000 378'.002'07 C99-901585-0

Cover design by Raoul Ollman

BLACK ROSE BOOKS

C.P. 1258	2250 Military Road	99 Wallis Road
Succ. Place du Parc	Tonawanda, NY	London, E9 5LN
Montréal, H2W 2R3	14150	England
Canada	USA	UK

To order books in North America:

(phone) 1-800-565-9523 (fax) 1-800-221-9985

In Europe: (phone) London 44 (0)20 8986-4854 (fax) 44 (0)20 8533-5821

Our Web Site address: http://www.web.net/blackrosebooks

A publication of the Institute of Policy Alternatives of Montréal (IPAM)

Printed in Canada

ACKNOWLI

The honor roll of friends, co-workers and students who have helped to improve this book is now almost as long as the list of villains who have provoked it. While most of the latter will receive their due in the pages that follow, I should like to take this moment to applaud all those who shared their wisdom, experience and expertise with me at a time when I needed it most.

So thank you Bill and Ben Livant (who were there from the start), Jack Barbalet, Mark Roelofs, John Ehrenberg, Michael Brown, Michael Parenti, Vincente Navarro, John McMurtry, Ira Shor, Leah Haus, Mitchell Cohen, Milton Polsky, Izzy Silver, Paul Gullen, Jon Birnbaum, Ed Vernoff, Frances Golden, David Harvey, Joe Murphy, Howard Sherman, Christine Harrington, Marilyn Laporte, Jim O'Connor, Savas Michael, Peter Haymens, John Ahliger, Leo Panitch, Paul Livant, Zack Brown, Joel Cohen, Rick Kuhn, Andrew Ross, Craig Stanley, John Meumaier, and the many others who I am forgetting. (Sorry) And thanks, too, to the 4-500 students in my classes over the last ten years who tested different versions of my test book and helped bring it up to snuff. And a profound thanks to the inspired band of radical cartoonists who have given me permission to use some of their best work: Jennifer Berman, Tulie Kupferberg, Charles Rodriguez, Mike Konopacki, Fred Wright, Carol Simpson, Rick Flores, Clay Bennett, Kirk Anderson and, especially, Gary Huck.

Finally, how can I not mention Paule, my wife, and Raoul, our son, who as always lived and laughed and suffered through it all? While Paule is at work fine-tuning my conscience, sensibility and taste (it's an ongoing job), Raoul enjoys special access to my unconscious from which he lifted the Holy Trinity found on the wonderful cover that he designed for this book. To get a better sense of what they have to put up with—and why I can never thank them enough (though I shall continue to try)—you might have a glance at the Ollman family portrait that graces the end of this work.

A big bear hug to you all. I only hope that *How to Take an Exam...and Remake the World*—by actually helping young people improve their skills in both—makes you feel that all the time and attention you gave to this oddest of "odd couples" was worthwhile.

For further information on Bertell Ollman, including a complete list of publications, see: www.nyu.edu/projects/ollman

INTRODUCTION

It is every student's dream come true: a test with ten True-False questions, where you know beforehand that the right answer to every question is True. And, if you forget, all the correct answers are written on the back of the sheet. Should you still fail, you can take the exam again and again on the same day until you pass. This is the official test to get a hand gun in the state of Michigan, whose major city, Detroit, has been called the "murder capitol" of the U.S. If all your exams are like this one, you can throw this book away right now. If not, some of the exam hints I've collected in the following pages could prove very useful. There's one problem and one catch.

I've taken hundreds of exams as a student and may have given even more in the thirty-five years that I've been a professor. In the course of all this, I've acquired an enormous exam lore. But, to tell you the truth, I don't feel any strong urge to share it with you. That's the problem. What I really would like to do is to tell you about capitalism, the system by which we produce and distribute the wealth of our society, but I suspect that most of you couldn't care less about what I have to say on this topic. Yet, you'd probably like to hear my exam advice. So: *Let's Make a Deal.* That's the catch.

I'll tell you what you need to know in order to write the best possible exams if you lend an ear to my account of capitalism. This book will be our "deal." My pledge: you get advice that is almost certain to raise your grades in virtually any subject area. My price: I get to harangue you—lightly, nothing that draws blood, not yours anyway—about what really concerns me. Okay? Except, since I know that many students cheat if given half the chance, I've not been so foolish as to divide the material by chapter. Instead, what you really want to hear is thoroughly mixed with up what I really want to tell you. Exam hints will appear at the start, in the middle and at the end of pages devoted to political exposé, and nothing in the style or size of print will offer a clue as to what's what. The book is organized rather like a fruit and nut cake, and to get at the fruit you've got to eat the nuts.

"Unfair!" you holler. That's right. The best thing you have going for you is the raw nerve that tells you when something isn't fair. It's also the best thing going for us, since we are all part of the same society. Well, what is and isn't fair, why it isn't, and what can be done about it is just what I want to talk to you about. And if I have to be a little unfair myself in order to get your attention, so be it.

In what follows, then, exam hints and political facts and ideas play off one another like contrasting themes in a musical fugue, with numbered intermissions called only when I think you need a break. Still, as in Bach's fugues, there is a slow build-up, an eventual mingling of themes, and a final crescendo. You may be in for a bumpy beginning, but let yourself go with the rhythm, and you'll learn how to dance to it soon enough.

ONE

‡ There are four main kinds of examinations: factual (including true/false, multiple choice, fill in the blank, short answer), essay, oral, and practical (experiment and other controlled exercises). In what follows, you will find helpful hints for all of them as well as on how to study for an exam.

Here is an actual radio transcript released by the U.S. Chief of Naval Operations (October 10, 1995):

> Station One: Please divert your course 15 degrees to the north to avoid a collision.
> Station Two: Recommend you divert your course 15 degrees to the south to avoid a collision.
> Station One: This is the Captain of a U.S. Navy ship. I say again, divert your course.
> Station Two: No, I say again, you divert your course.
> Station One: This is the aircraft carrier Enterprise. We are a large warship of the U.S. Navy. Divert your course now.
> Station Two: This is the Puget Sound Lighthouse. It's your call.

Well, is it the U.S.S. Enterprise that is heading for the rocks, or the "free" enterprise system of the U.S.? This book is intended to help you find out. And when you do, just remember, on this one, "It's *your* call."

‡ A friend once asked the American humorist, James Thurber, "How is your wife?" "As compared to what?" he replied. In Essay and Oral Exams, you will probably be asked to make judgements of various kinds. Most judgements of size, goodness, strength, beauty, etc. make use of a comparison, whether stated or implied. "As compared to what (or whom, or when)?" is a question you should often ask yourself. Making your object of comparison explicit and explaining why it is the relevant one in this case is a crucial though often neglected step in clarifying judgments and convincing others of them.

"Go inherit your own money!"

A young reporter asked a leading businessman how he made his first million. "It was really quite easy," answered the businessman. "I had five cents, and with it I bought an apple. I spend the evening polishing it, and the next day I sold it for ten cents. With that I bought two apples. I spent the evening polishing them, and the next day I sold them for twenty cents. With that I bought four apples. I spent the evening polishing them, and the next day I sold them for forty cents." And he continued in this way until he got to $12.80, at which point he added: "And it was then that my wife's father died and left us a million dollars."

It was said of George Bush (senior) that he was born on third base and thought he'd hit a triple. Forget the computer nerds who made it big in Silicon Valley; they are the exceptions. George Bush is the rule.

‡ True/False Exams: For those occasions where you don't have a clue as to the right answer, here are some statistics that may help in your guessing. A study by H.E. Hawkes, E.F. Lindquist, and C.R. Mann found that in statements containing the word "all," four out of five were false; in statements containing the word "none," four out of five were false; and in statements containing the word "always," three out of four were false. Whereas, in statements containing the word "some," four out of five were true; and in statements containing the word "generally," three out of four were true. They also found that the longer the statement, the more likely it is to be true.

Assuming that the readers of this book are typical of the mass of students in our capitalist world, there are some among you who in the years to come are going to commit suicide, or become drug addicts and alcoholics, or spend years as derelicts or in prison, and others, the luckier ones, will just lose your jobs and homes, or never get a good job or a decent home, and take your anger and frustration out in bouts of depression or in violence against your spouses and children. I'm going to tell you something that could save you from these horrible fates. Listen closely. *You are not guilty!* The conditions that are responsible for most of your suffering are not your fault; nor is it a matter of God's will, or of bad luck. Instead, most of what may one day drive you over the edge is due to this simple fact: *The Game is Rigged!* You never had a fair, let along equal, chance, and you won't. "Equality of Opportunity" is only a designer's label on the Emperor's new clothes. This is capitalism's dirty little secret. Once you know this secret and understand where and how it has been hidden, you can stop punishing yourself and your loved ones, and join in the struggle to change the rules of the game.

‡ In Essay Exams, it is generally wise to tackle your second best question first. If you answer the question you know most about first, there is a danger you will write too long and not leave enough time for other questions. Also, it takes a little while to warm up in an essay exam, and leaving the question you know most about for second increases the likelihood of doing your best on it. One of the worst answers I wrote on any exam was on the very question that I had been hoping would be there. I pounced on it immediately, but because I had so much to say it was very hard to finish. Then, noticing how little time I had left for the rest of the exam, I began to panic, and botched up the conclusion. I still have nightmares about this one.

After struggling and sacrificing through four or more years of university, you are ready to start a "career." Welcome to the world of part-time, temporary, "flexible," low paying, no benefit jobs, assuming you're lucky enough to find any job at all. It is estimated that over 30% of the work force is now part-time, and a majority of the new jobs created are now part-time and/or temporary. The owner of one agency that supplies temps and part-timers for businesses unashamedly admits we are creating a "new American sweat shop" made up of "disposable and throw-away workers." (*New York Times*, March 13, 1993) Is this what you've been preparing for?

In Bombay, India recently, the city government decided to do a major clean up and advertised for seventy jobs as rat catcher. There were 40,000 applicants, of whom half were college graduates. Just another piece of Third World exotica? Or a chilling glimpse of what life in New York (and Toronto, and London) will be like five to ten years down the road?

IGOR KOPELNITSKY

‡ In Oral Exams, most questions are composed on the spot, which means that they can be very vague and even contradictory. An otherwise brilliant professor with whom I often worked needed two or three verbal whacks at what he was thinking before anyone knew what he was talking about. Yet, again and again, students, who were too respectful of authority, assumed his first words had to make sense, and fell all over themselves trying to respond. The other professors present always felt very sorry for the poor student, whose self-confidence would begin to disintegrate right before our eyes, but there was nothing we could do. So, in an oral exam, don't assume that when a question is unusually difficult the fault is yours. Ask for a clarification. Be sure you know exactly what is being asked before you start to answer.

> "Take the bosses of the world's 1,000 largest companies, accounting for 4/5 of the world's industrial output, and 33 national leaders, including the president of the United States. Assemble them in a secluded Swiss ski resort, and then surround them with gun toting police. Is it any wonder that the annual meeting of the World Economic Forum in Davos this week has become, to some, a sign that there is a global economic conspiracy perpetuated by the white men in dark suits who run the world's multi-national corporations? Many people—and not just the folk with ponytails and placards who disrupted last December's meeting of the World Trade Organization in Seattle—now think of multi-nationals as more powerful than national states, and see them as bent on destroying livelihoods, the environment, left-wing political opposition and anything else that stands in the way of their profits." (*Economist*, Jan 29, 2000)

The otherwise respectable *Economist* is quick to deny that this is true—chiefly by claiming that multi-nationals are a force for good—but the cat has been let out of the bag.

‡ What's called "education" has taken many different forms over the centuries, just as its content has varied from A to Z, depending not only on what was known at the time but on the skills and personal qualities the rulers of each society wished to inculcate into their subjects. So in ancient Athens, for example, rhetoric occupied the central place on the curriculum. While teachers in Sparta were more likely to give practical instruction in swordsmanship and lectures on military valor. In medieval Europe, it was theology that received most of the attention. Yet, students everywhere probably believed that the kind of education they got is what "learning" is and has to be.

But once education is relativized in this way, two questions arise: 1) why do those who have power in our modern capitalist society want you to learn what you do and in the way(s) you do it? Given our special concern in this book, this translates into: Why so many exams? And, 2) starting from your own needs and interests, what would you like to learn and how would you like to learn it? Here are a couple of Life-Exam questions worth taking a few days/weeks/years to mull over. Helping you answer them would be my idea of a "good education."

Between 1983-1997, the productivity of American workers went up 17%, while their share of the wealth they produced went down 3.1%. They made more, but got less. Have you ever wondered what is fueling the rapid rise of values in the stock market? According to the English newspaper, *The Observer*, you need look no further:

> "The market is not rising on a bubble of fictions but on the rock-hard foundations of the spoils of class war." *(Jan 2, 2000)*

Of this new wealth, 85.5% has gone to the richest 1% of the population (268 of whom are billionaires), because they own 88% of all U.S. stocks and bonds. It appears that the well publicized increase in the number of people who own a few shares, either directly or through their pension funds, has had very little effect on the distribution of wealth in the country.

The same thing is happening in other capitalist countries. In England, for example, the wealth of the richest 200 people has doubled in the last ten years. Moving to a still more select circle, according to a U.N. Report, the richest 200 people in the world have doubled their wealth in the last four years. We also learn here that if these super-rich donated only 1% of their wealth, we could provide free primary education to every child in the world.

‡ In Multiple Choice Exams, when forced to guess, you can usually pass up choices that are very much alike, since no teacher wants to face a dozen angry students who can't understand why the answer they gave is wrong if it sounds—to them, at least—just like the answer said to be the correct one. On the other hand, if two answers are exact opposites, it is generally an indication that one of them is right, since few teachers would bother to think up the opposite to a wrong answer that is also wrong.

Despite popular myth, the U.S. does not do anything like as well providing for its ordinary citizens as it does in creating billionaires. Though it still produces far more wealth than any other country, the U.S. has fallen out of the top twenty on the U.N.'s Quality of Life Index, which includes such things as literacy, life expectancy, infant mortality, social services, and average income. A recent World Health Organization study (June, 2000) that graded countries on how well they met the health needs of their populations placed the United States 37th—yes, 37th!

There are, of course, many things where the U.S. is Number One in the world. Here's a short list: homicides (among young men, its twenty times higher than in Western Europe), military expenditures, drug consumption, prison population, financial bailouts for failing capitalists, and national debt. When was the last time you took an exam when one of these facts was the right answer? Yet, there can't be too many things that are more important for students to know, that is if we are to set our social house in order. You might want to keep track of how many of the facts and ideas in this book have ever found their way into your exams on any subject.

‡ In Studying for an exam, you are a little in the position of the cook in a restaurant who is waiting to receive an order from a customer. You can't prepare the order ahead of time because you don't know what it will be (you don't know the exact questions that will be asked). So the best you can do is to stock up on the ingredients required by the dishes that are on the menu, taking special care not to run short of those that are used in several dishes. In Essay and Oral exams, no ingredient is likely to prove more important in developing good answers for a variety of questions than brief, sharp definitions of the key concepts in the field. Like the cook, you must make sure that there is enough of this particular ingredient on hand to meet all requests.

MEMORIAL SERVICE OF AN INDUSTRIALIST

What the Minister Says:	What He Means:
• Not for him the easy way of retirement	• President of the company long after he became senile
• Not everyone had the good fortune to be admitted to his company of friends...	• Everyone hated him
• Never let family ties stand in the way of public duties	• Even his family hated him
• ...a man of strong loyalties	• Prejudiced

What the Minister Says (cont'd:	**What He Means (cont'd):**
• He retained the uncompromising blunt honesty of his Northern stock	• Racist
• He gave special consideration to his women employees needs	• Notorious for sexual harassment
• ...by no means oblivious to convivial aspects of life	• Drank like a fish
• He possessed a fund of genial anecdotes	• Bored everybody with tired jokes
• ...devoted a long career to unostentatious service	• Even the management forgot he existed
• This is neither the time nor place to speak of his accomplishments	• He's not paying my salary anymore

Paul Buhl, with apologies to Max Shulman

Now you try it. Your newspapers and textbooks—perhaps even your professor's lectures—are full of statements begging for such deconstruction.

‡ In True/False Exams, there are usually more true than false statements if only because it takes extra time and imagination to come up with statements that are both credible and false. Teachers are very rushed, and never more so than when making up and marking exams. Thus, they are prone to take short-cuts. Knowing what these are likely to be puts you one up on the odds.

Idealism, American style (now percolating out to the rest of the globe), is the belief that it is possible to go into a Chinese restaurant, order pizza, and actually get it. For most of our compatriots, it is only a matter of wanting it badly enough, believing you'll succeed, willing it—banging the table, if need be—and refusing to take "no" for an answer. Whatever we get (or don't get), it's all up to us as individuals. Isn't that what we're taught?

Save your breath. You can hang around a Chinese restaurant all week, and be as obnoxious as you like, but they still won't bring you a pizza. Why? Because pizza is not on the menu. Society, too, offers each of us a menu, and the choices we have in any area of life are restricted to what's on that menu. One can never choose what is not there to be chosen. Marxism, at its simplest, can be viewed as the "science of menus," analyzing the different menus available to different social classes (you didn't think they eat what you do?), how these menus get drawn up and how they change, and what we can do—but only together—if we don't like the "diet" to which we have been condemned. Pizza anyone?

‡ If you were studying a military dictatorship, in Myamar for example, and discovered that almost all of the members of the boards of trustees of their universities were generals, would you be justified in drawing certain conclusions about the nature of education in that country? You'd be dumb not to, right? Well, in the United States, it's businessmen, generally big businessmen and their lawyers, who dominate university boards of trustees.

Are these the most learned people in our society? The most public spirited? Because, in most cases, they aren't even paid for their services. Well, what are they doing there? What's in it for them, and how does that affect your education, even your exams? Perhaps there are students in Myamar who have never asked themselves this kind of question, but somehow I doubt it.

The Hollywood producer, Samuel Goldwyn, said, "Sincerity is everything. If you can fake that, you've got it made." One of the actors who worked for him learned this lesson so well that he went on to become President of the United States.

"Have we gone beyond the bounds of reasonable dishonesty?" —C.I.A. in a memo made available in General Westmoreland's libel suit relating to the Viet Nam War

Henry Luce, founder of *Time Magazine*, ordered his "The March of Time" newsreel company to use "fakery in allegiance to the truth whenever necessary."

"Bull permeates everything." —Lee Atwater, former GOP Chairman. He would know.

"In a time of universal deceit, telling the truth is a revolutionary act."

—George Orwell

MIND GULAG

‡ Hold everything. Before you go any further, I have a little test for you. It's a game I call "Mind Gulag," and it's meant to determine how much of your mind is already under enemy occupation. Prizes will be awarded at the end.

Answer True or False

1. Human beings are basically greedy and selfish.
2. The rich deserve what they have, because they earned it.
3. The poor also deserve what they have, because they haven't tried hard enough to improve their lot.
4. There have always been rich and poor, and always will be.
5. For democracy to exist, it is enough that two parties contest in elections, and that people are not coerced to vote for either one of them.
6. We are free as long as the state does not restrain us from doing what we want to do.
7. The American Government has been a major force promoting freedom and democracy around the world.
8. Most Americans are middle class.
9. Most workers are satisfied with their conditions and would never go on strike if not stirred up by outside agitators.
10. Socialism is what they had in the Soviet Union.

Now give yourself ten points for every time you answered *True*. Add up the total. Here are your prizes. Those who scored 0-30 win an Albert Einstein Medal for Critical thinking. Take an extra medal if you know that Einstein was a socialist. If you have a score of 40-70, you receive a Tiresias Pin (with points on both ends) indicating you can go either way. While those who racked up a count of 80-100 win a Ronald Reagan Gulag of the Mind Banner, which doubles as a blindfold, painted in red, white and blue. All prizes will be given out along with your college degree when you graduate. After all, who has done more to help you win your prize than your teachers?

(P.S. There is also a little test waiting for you at the end of this book: *no peeking*. I'll take full responsibility for how well/badly you do on that one.)

Everyone understands that in tough neighborhoods one has to become street-wise in order to survive. The university environment contains its own set of dangers. To help you overcome the worst of them I am trying to make you exam-wise, which is but the version of street-wise adapted to the perilous institution in which you are pursuing your degree. The traps may differ from one sector of life to the next, but the need for a cool appraisal of the dangers, knowing how those in charge think, sensing the options and, above all, good timing never does, not if you want to survive.

In letting you in on the secret of exams, I have also tried to make you street-wise about our system as a whole, because it isn't smart to put all your efforts into gaining access to a building that is even now falling down about your ears. The trick is to balance what you have to do well now, inside the parameters in which you find yourself, with a struggle to expand these parameters to take in all your human needs. There is no need to settle for mediocrity either inside or outside the class room.

Like *Zen and the Art of Motorcycle Maintenance*, a fashionable Bible among college youth a generation ago, *How to Take an Exam...and Remake the World* offers tips for all of life, except the underlying theme of my book is: RESIGNATION SUCKS. So get hip, get smart, get street-smart, watch out for open manhole covers, and let's get down to cases.

TWO

Do you keep falling asleep in class? Here is a way to change all that.

BULLSHIT BINGO

How to play: Check off each block when you hear the word during a class. When you get five blocks horizontally, vertically or diagonally, stand up and shout: *BULLSHIT!*

Paradox	**Compassionate Conservative**	**Downsizing**	**Department of Defense**	**There Is No Alternative (T.I.N.A.)**
Democratic Capitalism	**Out of the Loop**	**Equality of Opportunity**	**Didn't Inhale**	**It's Only Human Nature**
Reverse Discrimination	**Free Trade**	**Corporate Responsibility**	**National Interest**	**All Things Being Equal...**
Flexible Work	**Win-Win**	**Consumer Sovereignty**	**Middle Class**	**Environmental Protection Agency**
	(Insert	your own	favorites)	

With thanks to Kampfer

Testimonials from satisfied players:

> What a gas. School will never be the same for me after my first win. —David D., Florida
>
> The atmosphere was tense in the last political science class as fourteen of us waited for the fifth box. —Catherine L., Atlanta
>
> The professor was stunned when eight of us screamed 'BULLSHIT' for the third time in two hours. —Jack W., Boston

‡ In Essay and Oral Exams, radical students face a unique problem. It is not only that most teachers will disagree with the content of your answers, but they will have a lot of difficulty understanding what you have to say. The problem lies chiefly in the assumptions made and the language used by radicals (or, conversely, by your non-radical teacher, but then it's you taking the exam). The stopgap solution is to make as few assumptions as possible and to avoid using distinctively radical language unless absolutely necessary, and only then after carefully defining the term(s). It is simply that an exam is not the ideal occasion for laying out one's world view. If one follows some of the suggestions made in this book, however, it should be possible for radical students to do well on most exams while remaining true to their convictions. Admittedly, my experience at N.Y.U., which is smack in the middle of America's most cosmopolitan city, may have made me more optimistic in this regard than I would be if I were teaching elsewhere.

The recent earthquake in Los Angeles has proven a boon to that city's economy. How can that be? Didn't the quake destroy billions of dollars in property and disrupt thousands of businesses as well as kill and maim hundreds of people? Of course it did, but it also led to public and private investment of over $15 billion for rebuilding what was destroyed, and that provided jobs and incomes for many people who had neither before. Welcome to one of the miracles of capitalism: destruction pays.

Wars used to provide the boost our economy needs, but, given the current size of the economy, little wars are too small, and, with the weapons available, really big ones like World War II might prove too much for the planet. Earthquakes, on the other hand, seem to be just about right in their degree of destructiveness. Now if we could only arrange to spread them out more equitably over the whole country. It's just not fair for California to get all the big ones. Alternatively, we could look for another way to unlock the stored wealth of our society. Unless, of course, you think there is something natural, or rational, or ethical to wait for more and bigger earthquakes to help solve the country's social problems.

‡ In All Exams, the Golden Rule is to write as clearly as possible. With a large pile of exams to correct, nothing is more annoying than having to read the paper of someone who takes him/herself for a M.D. writing prescriptions. There is also the connection many teachers make between sloppy writing and sloppy thinking. The cost to the student is almost always a lower grade. On the other hand, in high school, I had a friend who would write indecipherably whenever he didn't know the answer. Since the teacher couldn't understand what he was saying, he figured he had a 50/50 chance of getting a better grade than he would have otherwise. I don't think the odds are that high, but it seems to have worked for my friend, who is now writing undecipherable prescriptions as a real doctor.

The popular media are full of stories about capitalists, but you'll notice that the term "capitalist" is hardly ever used. Instead, the owners of industry are referred to as "entrepreneurs," or "businessmen," "industrialists" and "employers" (never "un-employers," though they also un-employ workers). In Holland, the same people are called "work givers" and "social partners." All these names hide the real basis of the capitalists' power, which is ownership of the means of production, distribution and exchange, and the purpose for which they are used, which is making a profit, in sum all that makes capitalists different from other ruling classes in earlier periods of history.

Apparently, the term "capitalist," with its focus on owning, a passive state, and on maximizing profits, with all its anti-social implications, cuts too close to the bone for comfort. So a perfectly good technical term is left to radicals (simply uttering the term "capitalist" is enough to have oneself labeled a radical in some circles) and, interestingly enough, to capitalists themselves when talking to each other. The business press, for example, is full of references to "capitalist." The capitalists, it appears, are not afraid of calling a spade a spade in private, but they would just as soon have the rest of us think of them as people who do something a bit more useful.

‡ In Essay Exams, given the limited amount of time, it is very helpful if you can suggest that you know more than you're able to say. While name dropping may be socially unacceptable, it does have a place in exams, and the same holds for books and even lines of argument that you don't have time to pursue. My colleague Mark Roelofs has just reminded me of the Tom Lehrer song that says if stealing from one book is called plagiarism, stealing from twelve is considered research. But be careful not to over-do it. Don't allow these "asides" to become the main body of your answer. If an Oral Exam follows the written one, there is a good chance that you will be asked to comment on some of the people and books that you mentioned, so only bring them in if you really know them.

But aren't we all "middle class?" The idea of the middle class is so much sand thrown in our eyes to keep us from seeing the most important division in society, which is between the capitalists (those who own the means of production, distribution and exchange—and who make up the bulk of the very rich, along with the occasional sports hero and movie star) and the workers (those who work for them). The capitalists can't be more than a couple of percent of the population. To disguise the obscenity of so few people having so much wealth and power, and also their vulnerability in a society where all their workers have the vote, it is they who have manufactured the myth of a largely middle class America, in which life styles and attitudes become the main factors determining social class. As part of this, the capitalists also want desperately that workers who wear white collars to work think of themselves as "employees," "technicians," "assistants," "staff," "junior executives," indeed anything but workers.

Yet, if workers are people who are hired and fired by others, who also set their tasks, wages/salaries and work conditions, then there are more workers today than ever before. Whereas self-employed professionals and entrepreneurs made up 40% of the economically active population in the U.S. a century ago, they account for less than 10% today. Most of those engaged in similar activities now are employed by others, which makes them part of the working class, broadly construed, whether they know it or not, and whether they choose to save some of their money in the stock market or not. The fact that the number of workers in industry in the U.S. is at an all time low of 23.8% of the labor force has been used to mask the great increase in the number of wage and salary workers of all kinds. As of 1999, they account for 89.6% of the active labor force, which puts us in the lead among advanced capitalist countries, all of which have experienced the same decline in the number of industrial workers and the same growth in the working class overall.

After graduation, the great majority of students will find themselves in this working class, if they are not there already in virtue of their summer or part-time job, or as members of families whose breadwinners are workers. Therefore, it is in your interests—your class interests—that you recognize that the often repeated claim that the working class in America is in the process of disappearing is a myth promoted by those who can't afford—politically can't afford—to have a growing number of people think of themselves as workers.

"If you think this is bad, you haven't worked in a non-union shop."
George La Mendola, reprinted from New Masses, June 4, 1940

‡ How subjective is the grading process? In 1912, Daniel Stark and Edward Elliot sent two English essays to 200 high school teachers for grading. They got back 142 grades. For one paper, the grades ranged from 50 to 99; for the other, the grades went from 64 to 99. But English is not an "objective" subject, you say. Well, they did the same thing for an essay answer in mathematics and got back grades ranging from 28 to 95. Though most of the grades they received in both cases fell into the middle ground, it was evident that a good part of any grade was the result of who marked the exam and not of who took it.

Perhaps even more problematic, other studies have shown that the same teacher tends to grade differently depending on how he/she is feeling, the time of the day, how good or bad was the paper just before yours (following a really excellent paper generally results in a lower grade than you would have received otherwise), and whether yours is the first or last paper to be corrected.

With so much of one's grade dependent on the whims, moods and fancies, both conscious and unconscious—to which one must then add biases—of your teacher, it may seem that exam strategies have little to do with the outcome. On the contrary, it is just because of the high subjective content in the grading process that the way in which you present your answer can have such an impact. It is widely understood that when looking for certain jobs, it is necessary to wear the "right" kind of clothes. Looking for a good grade on exams often demands as much.

No one should conclude from the above that the short answer test is necessarily more objective that the essay exam. This may apply to the correction process, but the biases of your teacher have already found their way into the exam through the very choice of questions, their phrasing, and—where it applies—in the number and kind of answers offered. By choosing a short answer exam over an essay exam, the teacher has also revealed his/her bias in favor of uniformity and against creativity and variety. In sum, once you take up your pen, there is no way to escape the world constructed by your examiners, but there are ways to maximize your chances of being a winner in that world.

OFFICE MEMO

This notice was found in the ruins of a London office building. It was dated 1852:

1. This firm has reduced the hours of work, and the clerical staff will only have to be present between the hours of 6:00 a.m. and 7:00 p.m. weekdays.
2. Clothing must be of a sober nature. The clerical staff will not disport themselves in raiment of bright colors, nor will they wear hose unless in good repair.
3. Overshoes and topcoats may not be worn in the office, but neck scarves and head-wear may be worn in inclement weather.
4. A stove is provided for the benefit of the clerical staff. Coal and wood must be kept in the locker. It is recommended that each member of the clerical staff bring four pounds of coal each day during the cold weather.
5. No member of the clerical staff may leave the room without permission from the supervisor.
6. No talking is allowed during business hours.
7. The craving for tobacco, wine or spirits is a human weakness, and as such is forbidden to all members of the clerical staff.
8. Now that the hours of business have been drastically reduced, the partaking of food is allowed between 11:30 a.m. and noon, but work will not on any account cease!
9. Members of the clerical staff will provide their own pens. A new sharpener is available on application to the supervisor.
10. The supervisor will nominate a senior clerk to be responsible for the cleanliness of the main office and the supervisor's private

office. All boys and juniors will report to him 40 minutes before prayers and will remain after closing hours for similar work. Brushes, broom, scrubbers and soap are provided by the owners.

11. The owners recognize the wisdom of the new labor laws, but will expect a great rise in output to compensate for these near Utopian conditions.

The first thing that strikes us on reading this office memo from 1852 is how much capitalism has changed. The second thing that strikes us on reading this memo is just how little has changed. Check your own experience for both. We will return to the crucial question of what has changed in capitalism and what hasn't later in the book.

‡ In Multiple Choice Exams, such loaded expressions as "stupid," "nonsensical," "ugly," etc. are unlikely to be part of the right answer. Technical terms that the teacher never used in class are also generally a good indication to avoid choosing sentences in which they appear. Similarly, funny answers are unlikely to be the right ones. Teachers often waste alternative answers to display their sense of humor. For teachers, it can be a way to retain their sanity while making up exams, and, perhaps, unconsciously, a reach for solidarity with the suffering student.

On September 29, 1991, the *New York Times Sunday Magazine* ran twenty four pages of ads for expensive fur coats. It was that moment in the year to let those who could afford them know where they could be found: mink, chinchilla, sable, fox. "Quintessentially chic, undeniably fabulous...If a woman wants a fur, it's her right...all the luxury you've longed for." Without any transition, or sense of shame, the very next article in the magazine presented a six page spread on poverty in New York, in which photos taken one hundred years ago were compared with those taken today. The conclusion of the article was that along with new complications added by guns, drugs and race, poverty today is both "deeper and more ubiquitous" than the poverty of an earlier time.

For example, half of the children born that year (and this year too) will find themselves on welfare at one time or another before they turn eighteen.

‡ In Essay Exams, when you make an important generalization, it is good form to accompany it with at least one exception (assuming there are some). This is usually taken as a sign that you know the subject very well. If you can then explain—briefly—how that exception came about, that's a slam dunk answer.

"Tonto, Tonto, we're surrounded by Indians." Do you remember this one? And Tonto's response: "Who's 'we,' Lone Ranger?" I'm reminded of this exchange every time someone trots out an increase in the Gross National Product (G.N.P.) as evidence that life is getting better for everyone. However, the figures given for the G.N.P. just tells us how much wealth has been produced, not what it is made of (much of it is junk or worse: armaments, prisons, advertising) and not who gets it. It is also estimated that 45% of our G.N.P. goes to "transaction costs": banking, insurance, wholesale and retail trade, and accountants. This is much more than for any other country, and a huge 20% increase over what such groups took from the national pie one hundred years ago.

An increase in the G.N.P., which is the economic accomplishment that the Government boasts about more than any other, is perfectly compatible with large numbers of people and even a majority getting less than they did before. Faced with just that situation in Mexico and the public cynicism that it bred, an economic advisor to the President of Mexico was forced to admit, "Our challenge is to convince the people that the economy is as good as the numbers say." But people's lives tell them otherwise.

The next time one of our leaders (sic) or his economist sidekick uses the latest G.N.P. figures to convince you how well the country is doing, you can answer, "Who's 'we,' Lone Ranger?" Our rallying cry: "Take 'Con' Out of 'Economics.' "

‡ In Essay and Oral Exams, be careful not to begin more than a couple of answers with the same words. There are formulae that are useful in helping us to learn, but don't give your teacher the impression that without a particular word order you would be lost. Anything that makes you sound like a programmed android is to be avoided, since the best grades are reserved for humans.

The way the U.S. Government calculates official unemployment has undergone 30 adjustments since 1979, most of them—surprisingly—resulting in a fall in "unemployment." Thus, official unemployment statistics, as bad as they are—hovering around 5% in the U.S.—regularly understate the truth, chiefly because they don't count various categories of people who would like to have a regular full time job. They don't include part-time or temporary workers (working an hour a week or having a contract for a week's work are considered being employed); they don't include people who are so discouraged that they have given up looking for a job, or people, especially among the young, who are so pessimistic about finding one that they haven't started looking yet; they don't include people on training courses that go nowhere, or consultants, apprentices, independent contractors, pedlars, and failing farmers and small business-people, who would like to have the security of a full time job; they don't include many housewives and househusbands and people with various handicaps, who would like jobs if provisions were made to deal with their special concerns; they don't include early retired, soldiers, prisoners, bums and some students, who would prefer a full time job to what they're doing.

So how many people are unemployed? Obviously many times the number that we're given. We get some idea of what the number might be whenever there is a war with its open-ended call for more workers, at which point millions of people turn up for work who were never counted among the unemployed. They were always unemployed and after the war will be again, even though, once again, the official statistics will appear to deny it. For the Government, it is simply politically inadvisable (dangerous?) to admit that our system functions with so much waste, wasted labor, wasted wealth that such labor could create, and wasted lives of the people who are forced to go without both. Life Exam Question: if capitalism is so efficient, then why is it so wasteful?

A similar misuse of statistics occurs in counting the number of poor people in America. The deceptive techniques include setting the poverty line at a ridiculously low level ($17,050 for a family of four, which gives us *only* 35 million poor, including one out of every five children in the country—a more realistic figure of $25,000 would double the number of poor and, with that, the number of poor children); not taking adequate account of inflation, particularly as it effects basic necessities (which means that whatever money poor people get buys them less than it once did); and discounting the steady erosion of social services (which deprives many poor people of the medical, housing, educational, counseling, legal and child care benefits that may have eased their plight just a few years earlier).

Should you believe that poverty is a condition reserved for those who don't have jobs, you should also know that the "official" poverty rate for working families has gone up nearly 50% in the last two decades. Currently, of the approximately two million people who experience homelessness in the U.S. every year, that is among the desperately poor, 25-40% are employed but don't earn enough to afford a home. Life Exam Question: Who benefits from grossly underestimating the number of poor people in America?

‡ When your head is in the freezer and your feet are on the stove, the "average" is what tells you that the temperature of your stomach is just right. Got it? It could have been someone, who received such assurance, who first declared that there are three kinds of lies: simple lies, damned lies and statistics. Statistics are the worse lies, because they seem so, well, objective. Yet, it is relatively easy to use statistics (and charts and graphs) to derive grossly distorted conclusions from basically accurate data. It all depends on what aspect of the situation

one chooses to focus on, all that one takes as given ("All things being equal..."), how one determines averages, the definitions one accepts for key terms, what one presents as the base year (the time at which the process under examination is said to begin), how the figures are gathered, what are treated as relevant comparisons, and there are still other considerations.

Teachers are often less aware of the possible manipulations of statistics than they should be. Of this, too, you should be aware. In commenting on statistics used in an exam question, or quoting your own statistics in an answer, therefore, you should try to add at least something about its bias and one-sidedness as well as what it does *not* reveal (perhaps cannot reveal).

"When I feed the poor, they call me a saint. When I ask why they are poor, they call me a communist." —Brazilian Bishop, Dom Helder Camara.

Jesus condemned the rich just for being rich when there was so much poverty around, and said, "It is harder for a rich man to get into heaven than for a camel to pass through the eye of a needle." The early Church fathers frequently attacked the rich and their claims to be the legitimate owners of what they possessed.

According to Saint Basil, "The rich are like people who occupy a place in a theater and don't allow others to enter, treating as their own what was designed to be used by everybody. Because they are now in possession of what are common goods, they take these goods as their own."

Saint Jerome claimed, "The common opinion seems to be very true: the rich man is unjust, or the heir of an unjust one. Opulence is always the result of theft, if not committed by the actual possessor, then by his predecessor."

Saint Augustine, himself, pointed out, "The superfluidities of the rich are the necessities of the poor. Those who possess superfluidities, therefore, posses the goods of others."

Jesus Christ

WANTED FOR SEDITION, CRIMINAL ANARCHY, VAGRANCY, AND CONSPIRING TO OVERTHROW THE ESTABLISHED GOVERNMENT.

Dresses Poorly. Said To Be A Carpenter By Trade, Ill-Nourished, Has Visionary Ideas, Associates With Common Working People, The Unemployed And Bums.

Alias— Believed to be a Jew

Alias— 'Prince of Peace' 'King of the Jews' 'Son of Man' 'Light of the World' etc., etc.

Professional Agitator

Red Beard, marks on Hands and Feet— The Result of Injuries Inflicted By an Angry Mob Led By Respectable Citizens and Legal Authorities.

Except for the Liberation Theology Movement within the Catholic Church (no thanks to this Pope) and a smaller fringe among Protestants (most of them Black, like Martin Luther King), most Christians today are unaware of these teachings. Otherwise, it is hard to see how they could accept the capitalist order and still consider themselves Christians.

Was Martin Luther King reacting as a Christian or a socialist, or just being logical and common-sensical (or all of the above), when he said, "Why are there forty million poor people in America? When you begin to ask that question, you begin to question the capitalist economy...one day we must come to see that an edifice that produces beggars needs restructuring?" Comments such as these led J. Edgar Hoover, the long-time head of the F.B.I., to consider Reverend King the most dangerous "communist" in America.

And just in case you think such socialist sentiments are limited to the Christian religion, here is the Dalai Lama: "Of all the modern economic theories, the economic system of Marxism is founded on moral principles, while capitalism is concerned with only gain and profitability. Marxism is concerned with the distribution of wealth on an equal basis and the equitable utilization of the means of production. It is also concerned with the fate of the working classes—that is the majority—as well as with the fate of those who are underprivileged and in need; and Marxism cares about the victims of minority-imposed exploitation. For these reasons the system appeals to me, and it seems fair...The failure of the regime in the Soviet Union was, for me, not the failure of Marxism but the failure of totalitarianism. For this reason I think of myself as half-Marxist and half-Buddhist."

‡ In Oral Exams, professors know that students are nervous, and that this often leads to a proliferation of whatever verbal ticks the examinee already has, such as "you know," "like, I mean," "okay," "right," etc. While professors generally try not to be affected by the constant repetition of these meaningless expressions, you should

know that students who talk like this sound a lot less smart than they really are. So if you have one of these speech impediments (what else is it?), try to get rid of it—before the oral. At the exam, it helps to take a moment before answering any question—don't be afraid of the silence—since these expressions are often used to fill up time while one tries to think of something to say. It's rapid talkers who suffer most from this problem, so slowing down your delivery may help.

Letter to the New York Times, unpublished

July 1, 1979

To the Editor:

Question: What is the difference between the most advanced country in the world(ours) and a Third World country? Answer: While governments in the Third World try to build more hospitals, our leaders close down the ones we have. ("We can't afford them.") This is why our country is called "advanced."

I have just learned from an informed source at City Hall that as the next step on this ladder of advancement, Mayor Koch will reintroduce the "potlatch," the practice of burning large quantities of whatever one owns to celebrate a marriage. With people, especially New Yorkers, getting married so many times, the potlatch should go a long way to solve capitalism's problem of overproduction. If after this, we (sic) still cannot afford our wealth, there may be no alternative but to start burying people's worldly goods with them when they die. Though such an advance in civilization might require tidying up some religious doctrines, my source informs me that Mayor Koch and the business groups he represents are very impressed by what it would do to the market for cars and houses, not to mention pyramids.

And if, through all this, anybody protests they don't have enough, it simply shows their ignorance of capitalist economics.

Sincerely,

Prof. Bertell Ollman, Department of Politics, N.Y.U.

‡ For Short Answer Exams, you are usually expected to give the exact name/word/or phrase, but if you can't remember it, put down the general idea in your own words. Teachers will often give at least partial credit for this.

Who said the following: "The bourgeoisie...has been the first to show what man's activity can bring about. It has accomplished wonders far surpassing Egyptian pyramids, Roman aqueducts and Gothic cathedrals; it has conducted expeditions that put in the shade all former Exoduses of nations and crusades." Surprisingly, it's Karl Marx. No one surpasses Marx in his admiration for all the positive achievements of capitalism. Constantly reinvesting its surplus to produce still larger surpluses (unlike earlier civilizations where the ruling class consumed most of the surplus product), capitalism has created unheard of riches, with levels of science and technology to match. It has also helped to spread the ideas of freedom, equality and democracy across the globe, and, as compared to feudalism, made substantial progress in embodying one or another version of these ideas in its institutions. For all this, and more, capitalism deserves enormous credit. Yet, four questions cry out for answers:

1) What is the price in human suffering and in material destruction, including the despoilation of nature, that humanity has paid (and continues to pay) for these achievements?
2) Which groups—nations, races, genders and classes—have been forced to pay most of this price?
3) In resolving certain problems set by feudalism (like the need to industrialize) has capitalism created new problems (like growing inequality, industry produced unemployment, economic exploitation, social alienation, urban degradation, ecological devastation, etc.) for which it has no solutions? And,

4) Can we do better, that is with the help of all the industry, wealth, skills and knowledge that capitalism itself has provided,

can we organize society in a more rational manner in order to solve these very problems?

There is no contradiction, in other words, in believing, as Marx does, that capitalism helped humanity solve earlier problems, but that the problems which have arisen or gotten worse as a necessary part of its own development require another kind of solution.

‡ The same two-sided approach can be applied to exams. Compared to feudalism, where all the prized posts in society were distributed on the basis of "blood," the introductions of exams, which accompanied the rise of capitalism, marked a significant improvement. Where there was no equality of opportunity before, now there was some. The questions that remain to be answered, however, are:

1) How does the current system of exams reflect the power relations in capitalist society, where inequality and not equality is the rule?

2) What is the real contribution of exams, especially so many exams, to education?

3) Are exams mainly a way of choosing society's winners, or of preparing its far more numerous losers to accept uncomplainingly, the harsh fate that awaits them? And,

4) Can we do better, in other words: What would education without exams look like, and what other changes would have to occur to make such a reform possible?

Before trying to answer all these questions about exams and capitalism, take a moment to reflect on the words of that genuine American hero, Tom Paine:

> "Let them call me a rebel and welcome, I feel no concern from it; but I shall suffer the misery of devils, were I to make a whore of my soul."

THREE

The one thing that everyone can buy enough of these days is lies. The air is full of them, since the going currency is gullibility, and we all have enough of that. Looking for a philosophy of education that will help you survive in this situation? Try these on for size:

"Doubt everything." —René Descartes (but also Karl Marx)

"Seek simplicity, but distrust it." —Alfred North Whitehead (English philosopher)

"Education is a crap detector." —Ernest Hemmingway (It usually isn't, of course, but it should be.)

"I have never let my schooling interfere with my education." —Mark Twain

‡ One study of people who did poorly on exams found that they shared the following characteristics: 1) they run through directions and sometimes skip them altogether; 2) they resort to one-shot thinking; 3) they put little faith in reasoning as a way of solving problems; 4) if they don't perceive an answer immediately, they feel lost; 5) they operate on feelings and hunches; and 6) they rarely go back to reread or to clarify. If you recognize any of this in your own approach to exams, we have serious work to do. Hopefully, this book will provide an effective antidote to all this.

Astronomers reported a few years back that they had just discovered one of the largest concentration of galaxies and other matter ever found. It is being described as a "continent of galaxies." They are calling it the "Great Attractor," because it attracts matter very far from it. The mystery is why something so big and having such an important effect on our galaxy (and therefore on our solar system, and finally on our own planet) was not seen before. Astronomers generally focus on small segments of the sky, so when one astronomer was asked why no one had noticed the Great Attractor, his answer was that it is just because of its large size. "With this one, we could not see the forest for the trees...It was literally so big, covered so much of the sky that no one looked for it."

Capitalism is a similar kind of object. It exercises a strong effect on everything that goes on inside it, but like the Great Attractor, it's too big for most people to see. They are so busy focusing on the parts—inequality, biased government, power of money, feelings of alienation, etc.—that they never look to see what they are parts of. And our schools haven't offered much help. The article on the Great Attractor goes on to say that astronomers now realize that the size of objects that make up our universe is much larger than they had thought, and that our theories must be adjusted to take this into account. The same kind of readjustment is required as soon as we realize that the great variety of events and conditions that make up life in our society all reflect to one degree or another some truth about capitalist civilization.

But though some adjustment in our way of thinking is required, it is not always easy or comfortable to make. One astronomer is quoted as saying that the discovery of the Great Attractor is a "thorn in the side" of current theories, and that many of their defenders "were hoping it would go away." (*New York Times*, January 2, 1990) Defenders of mainstream theories that deal with existing social inequalities have adopted a similar stance toward the capitalist system in which these inequalities are found. But capitalism, like the Great Attractor, won't simply go away, so we need to adjust our thinking in order to better understand how this system effects our daily lives, our past and our possible futures. And for this, we need—for a starter—to bring capitalism into clearer view, as Marxism tries to do, and make it a major object of study.

‡ Complaining about exams may be most students' first truly informed criticism of the society in which they live, informed because they are its victims and know from experience how exams work. Students know, for example, that exams don't only involve reading questions and writing answers. They also involve forced isolation from other students, prohibition on talking and walking around and going to the bathroom, writing a lot faster than usual, physical discomfort, worry, fear, anxiety (lots of that) and often guilt. From their experience, many students are also aware that most education has become preparation for exams, that exams do a poor job of testing what students actually know, and that the correction and grading process is highly subjective and done by professors with whom they've had only minimal contact.

What student hasn't griped about at least some of these things? But it is just here that their criticism runs into a brick wall, because most students don't know enough about society to understand the role that exams—especially taking so many exams—play in preparing them to take their place in it.

Have you noticed how our vocabulary for cow changes when it is meat at the butcher's? The parts have names—"steak," "cutlet," etc.—which keeps us from recognizing what they are parts of. This enables us to forget the cow and eat the meat. Something very similar happens with the vocabulary that is applied to the different parts of society. With the larger picture safely out of sight, the part can be treated in ways that would not be possible if people were fully aware of its place and role, and therefore too meaning and importance, in the whole. It is this which sets up the landlord, for example, to charge a rent for what he calls his "property," and to dismiss its function as a home, a necessary condition of life, for those who live in it; referring to human beings as "employees" makes it easier for capitalists to fire them, since the personal and family relations of these people are temporarily blocked out; while labeling people "consumers" allows many to dismiss their lives as workers along with their need to earn enough money to be good consumers.

Like Humpty Dumpty, capitalism has been broken into so many pieces that it is almost impossible to see what they are pieces of. It's like hearing only a few sentences or only one side in a telephone conversation. What sense can we make of what's being said? This practice finds an echo in the universities, where knowledge itself is divided up and apportioned to different and often competing disciplines, each with its distinctive vocabulary and own set of methods. The result is widespread confusion over the nature of the whole. Yet, without a fix on the whole—and this applies as much to capitalism as to cows—it is impossible to grasp the place and function, and with them the greater meaning and importance, of any of the parts.

‡ In Multiple Choice Exams, note the different psychologies that underlay the answers, "All of the above," and "None of the above." I would expect the former to be favored by teachers who view the exam situation as but another chance to convey information on their subject. If I ever gave this kind of exam—which I don't—this would be the right answer more often than not. While "None of the above," since it usually follows choices that are almost right, strikes me as something that is more likely to be used by teachers who enjoy setting traps for students. So, if forced to guess, take a couple of seconds to decide which of these descriptions best fits your teacher.

The 19th century French socialist, Charles Fourier, detected something terribly perverse operating in our society "in which portions of the whole are in conflict and acting against the whole. We see each class," he said, "desire, from interest, the misfortunes of other classes, placing in every way individual interest in opposition to public good. The lawyer wishes litigations and suits, particularly among the rich; monopolists and forestallers want famine, to double or triple the price of grain; the architect, the carpenter, the mason want conflagrations that will burn down a hundred houses to give activity to their branch of business." He didn't mention undertakers, but you know what they want. In the 1970s, the *Wall Street Journal* ran a story on how this had been a bad year for small businessmen because there had been a slight increase in the minimum wage and a modest improvement in workers' safety rules.

In a system that gives each person a monetary interest in the misfortunes that befall others, many actually hope for such misfortunes, paying a price in guilt perhaps for what they can't help feeling. Is this a rational, ethical and psychologically healthy way in which to order our lives together? Or, you could write it off as just one of the many "paradoxes"—like earthquakes that bring prosperity—of which our society seems so blessed. A headline in the *International Herald Tribune* yesterday, for example, read: "Rise in Unemployment Delights the Market." (June 3, 2000)

‡ In an Oral Exam, don't be afraid to say, "I don't know," even a few times. This is par for the course, and generally accepted as such. The danger is to let such an admission throw you into a panic and start a downward spiral. No one there expects you to be able to answer every question, even for a top grade. And don't apologize and offer excuses: sounds too defensive. (Same applies to written exams) Just say you don't know or can't remember. You can add a "But...," and try to introduce what you do know that is related to what is being asked, though this tactic seldom works.

In the United States every year, 19,000 people are murdered but 56,000 are killed at work, far more than in any other industrial country. Yet, the media is full of accounts of murders, but devotes very little space/time to work related deaths and injuries. Is it any wonder that the U.S. is the only developed country that does not publish mortality statistics by class?

The problem is not that American workplaces are inherently more dangerous than those in other countries. Rather, our laws protecting workers' health are much too weak; government inspectors, who are supposed to check on whether these laws are kept, are far too few (there are about ten times as many inspectors working for the Fish and Wildlife Service as there are for OSHA, the agency that investigates workplaces); and the penalties for employers who break the law are ridiculously small. When 500 coal companies were caught tampering with the tests used to determine the amount of coal dust in their mines (Black Lung Disease kills and disables thousands of miners every year), they were given a citation accompanied by a $1,000 fine for every violation. For the companies caught, fines averaged about $10,000, which doesn't come close to the amount of profit each company made by breaking the law. Rather than receiving a fine, it sounds more like these capitalists were buying a license to kill and maim their workers in order to make a little more profit.

‡ A colleague told me of an outstanding student who gave a picture perfect account of Rousseau's theory of the social contract on an exam that he gave. Except the question that he asked was: "What were Rousseau's other contributions to politics besides the theory of the social contract?" She got an "F." Many students treat the beginning of an exam like the beginning of a foot race, and are off and running/writing as soon as they hear the starter's gun. But being quick off the mark is no assurance that one is proceeding in the right direction. Without doubt, the most common error students make in exams is that they answer a question other than the one the teacher asked.

While one of the biggest dangers is straying from the point, it is sometimes possible to affect what that point is, which is to say that sometimes you can interpret the question in a way that allows you to give the strong answer that you've prepared beforehand. "If we take 'freedom' to mean..." It's a trick that usually involves redefining a key word or two in a way that the teacher did not expect but is hard put to reject. You may well fall on your face, but if you succeed the rewards are great. Recommended for superior students only, and then only in courses given by open-minded teachers.

Capitalists don't only kill and maim their workers. They also kill and maim many of their customers, also unnecessarily, also in pursuit of higher profit. A *New York Times* headline (November 7, 1992) declaimed, "Data Shows General Motors Knew For Years Risk In Pickup Truck's Design." The toll here was over 300 deaths from 1983, when the fault was first recognized, to 1988, when—after many law suits and threats—G.M. agreed to correct it. Dow Corning knew for years that the silicon gel it implanted in the breasts of over one million women could be hazardous, but kept this information secret; Upjohn withheld equally disturbing data on it's sleeping pill, Halcion; Bolar, another pharmaceutical giant, mislabeled and adulterated eight of its drugs. And we haven't even arrived at the tobacco, firearms and tire industries.

How far will capitalists go to maximize their profits? Well, it depends on how much profit there is to be made. As Marx already pointed out 150 years ago, "With adequate profit, capital is very bold. A certain 10% will ensure its employment anywhere; 20% certain will produce eagerness; 50% positive audacity; 100% will make it ready to trample on all human laws; 300% and there is not a crime at which it will scruple, nor a risk it will not run, even to the chance of its owner being hanged. If turbulence and strife will bring a profit, it will freely encourage both."

‡ Question: "What is the difference between an apple and an elephant?" Answer: "I don't know." Punch line: "Well, I sure as hell won't send you to the store to buy apples." Yes, I know you've heard this joke before, but there is an important piece of exam wisdom to be extracted from it. By responding "I don't know," the person to whom the question is directed lays him/herself open to the insulting retort. But why does he answer in this way? Of course, he knows the difference between apples and elephants, but the question, he reasons, could not possibly be asking what it seems to. That would be too simple. It has to be a trick question. Some questions, in other words, are so easy that it's hard to believe they are not hiding something more complex and difficult.

A much less funny version of this joke is replayed time and again in Oral Exams, especially at the start. A sympathetic professor asks a ridiculously easy question, hoping in this way to relax the candidate. But the student can't believe that the question really means what it seems to. That would be too simple. There must be a trick. So the student sets out to look for it, falling all over himself and ruining his self-confidence in the process. Meanwhile, a couple of professors are thinking to themselves, "He doesn't even know *that.*" All of this could easily be avoided if students just realized that the first questions in an Oral Exam are likely to be as simple as they sound. So always start with the obvious answer. If the professor wants to take you into deeper water, he/she will do so.

Who said the following: "Bolshevism is knocking at our gates. We can't afford to let it in. We have got to organize ourselves against it, and put our shoulders together and hold fast. We must keep the worker away from red literature and red ruses; we must see that his mind remains healthy"? It's the same person who said, "The American system of ours, call it Americanism, call it capitalism, call it what you like, gives each and every one of us a great opportunity if we only seize it with both hands and make the most of it." Cat got your tongue? The great defender of capitalism turns out to be America's most famous gangster, Al Capone. (*Liberty Magazine*, 1929)

Do you think the ancient Greeks were trying to tell us something when they made Hermes the God of both businessmen and thieves?

'Amateurs!..'

‡ Are you ready for Exams Corrected by Machines? Well, you will be in just a moment. For it seems that machine corrected exams are not just coming; they have already arrived. And I'm talking about essay exams no less. Already two essay questions on the Graduate Management Admissions Test taken by about 200,000 business school applicants have been corrected by a machine, and you can be sure this is just the beginning. So what is the machine, which is called the "E-rater," looking for? Obviously—and admittedly—not for creative thinking. A spokesman for the company administering the test speaks about "the organization of ideas and syntactical structure," which the Kaplan Educational Center (a major test preparation company) has translated into: 1) start with a clear outline (sign of an organized answer); 2) use a lot of transitional phrases like "therefore," "since," and "for example" (sign of a structured answer); and, 3) don't hold back on the synonyms (sign of a strong vocabulary). (*New York Times*, January 27, 1999) Are you pleased that you are finally going to be graded "objectively?" (If so, maybe you deserve what you're about to get.)

THE MONTHLY RENT

19th century poem

by Bolton Hall

"God tempers the wind to the shorn lamb," said the deacon.

"I will shut the gate to the field, so as to keep him warm," said the philanthropist.

"The lambs we have always with us," said the wool broker.

"Lambs must be shorn," said the businessman. "Hand me the shears."

"We should leave him enough wool to make him a coat," said the profit sharer.

"His condition is improving," said the land owner, "for his fleece will be longer next year."

"We should prohibit cutting his flesh when we shear," said the legislator.

"But I intend," said the radical, "to stop this shearing."

The others united to throw him out. Then they divided the wool.

How do you think tigers are trained to jump through hoops at the circus? A little bit of whipping here, when they do it wrong, a little bit of raw steak there, when they do it right, and eventually they get it. Students too have to be trained to jump through hoops. It doesn't come natural or easy to them either.

Exams, lots of them, with curt, crisp orders that can't be questioned, and loaded down with threats of all sorts—an "F" and expulsion from school—that's the whip. A high grade and a good recommendation from the teacher—that's the raw steak. After a youth misspent playing such sadistic games, most students are ready to jump through any hoop held up by their future employer.

The French philosopher, Pascal, said if you make children get on their knees every day to pray, whatever they may start out thinking, they will end up believing in God. What applies to praying applies to taking exams. If you make students take so many exams, they will end up believing _________? You fill in the blank (my answer will come later). Just remember, we not only learn from what we read (books) and hear (lectures) but from what we do and what is done to us, from our experiences. Of these, our experiences are the most important, because they usually combine activity with perception and a stronger dose of emotions than accompanies just reading and listening on their own. Consequently, the form of education—in this case, frequent exams and our experience in taking them and studying for them—can be more influential on our thinking and feeling than the content of what is taught. What Marshal McLuhan said of T.V.—to wit, "The medium is the message"—also applies to exams. It is in this sense that exams, repeated exams, teach us far more than they test us.

FOUR

A joke goes around about a girl who asks her father, "Why is it so cold in the house?" "We don't have any coal," he says. "But why is there no coal?" she wants to know. "Because I lost my job in the coal mine," he replies. Still unsatisfied, she asks one more time, "And why did you lose your job?" To which he answers, "Because there is too much coal."

Except it's no joke. That's exactly why her father, and maybe yours as well, lost their jobs in the mines and in the factories and on the farms and in the offices. There is "too much." But "too much" for whom? Surely not for all the people who still need these products and services, often to the point of desperation. And not "too much" for the workers who want to continue making and providing them. Something is seriously out of whack here. Of course, if you're comfortable with this "paradox"—which is what our mass media insist on calling such nuttiness—just turn on a sitcom and tune me out. Otherwise, read on.

‡ On Factual Exams, it's almost always better to stick with your first answer unless you are sure it is wrong. This is because at some deep level people know more than they are fully conscious of. Hence, your initial answer, no matter how hesitant, is more likely to be right than your later correction. Wait. I'm beginning to have second thoughts. Have I overstated this point? No, I'll take my own advice, and stick with what I said first.

It often seems that what's called "politics" in our society consists of deciding what kind of diet to go on, exploring different self-help therapies, calling into the talk show of your choice, and voting for interchangeable politicians every few years. A similar approach to solving problems can be seen in society's treatment of the common cold. In 1990, the producers of cold and cough remedies introduced 48 new products that came in 85 different colors and sizes. The real differences between them ranged from slight to non-existent, and colds and coughs continue to plague us as before. But no matter, in our system, it's having a choice, any choice, even if it's between Tweedle Dee and Tweedle Dum (or is it *especially* if it's between Tweedle Dee and Tweedle Dum?) that counts.

People apparently feel that their problem is being addressed if they have a lot of solutions to choose from. This way if one doesn't work, they can move on to another. But if they are all versions of the same thing, and none of them work, then flooding us with choices is a way of hiding the fact that we really don't have any choice at all. The truth is that we're stuck— stuck with the same hamburgers under a dozen different labels, stuck with the same boring, stressful and low paying jobs no matter the employer, stuck with the same pap and drivel dispensed by all the main media outlets, stuck with the same cough syrup in a variety of oddly shaped bottles, and stuck with virtually identical politicians who serve the same business interests.

The *New York Times* (August 22, 1994) ran a story on the "paradox" (still another one) that many major corporations give large sums of money to both the Democrats and the Republicans. In way of explanation, Ken Dickerson, a vice president of the Arco Oil Company, said, they "regularly give to both parties, regardless of who is in power, as a matter of principle." Now you know what principle he means. In this situation, our only real choice is to get rid of the system, capitalism, which has been so successful in fooling people that they have lots of choices.

‡ Are you being forced to learn too many useless facts? The German philosopher, Nietzsche, said, "Knowledge taken in excess without hunger, even contrary to need, no longer acts as a transforming motive impelling to action." And maybe that's what it's all about. After all, a lot of the facts you learn help you to make choices, which—as we saw—offer no choice at all. Lenin said that 9/10 of what we learn is intended to leave no time for coming to grips with the 1/10 that is really important. If this is so, where does that leave all these exams?

Mayor Carty Finkbeiner of Toledo once suggested that the problem of noise pollution at the local airport could be resolved if we allowed only deaf people to live in the surrounding area. An equally bright idea is to turn the "right to pollute" into a commodity and allow the companies that pollute more than the law allows to buy the rights or "credits" of companies that pollute very little if at all. This way the big polluter is happy, because it can now pollute to its heart's content. The other companies are happy, because they've just made money for not doing what they didn't do anyway. And only the public is unhappy, because...(cough, cough, cough!). Be ready for a lot more of this scam.

There are, of course, some anti-pollution laws, but how do they work? According to Nikki Roy, a former Environmental Protection Agency (A.P.A.) regulator, a lot of the money that is spent on avoiding pollution goes into "toxic shell games." (*Daily Yomiuri*, Tokyo, August 11, 1994) Until recently, for example, steel plants were forbidden to dispose of waste water that contained certain toxic agents into rivers or lakes, but they were allowed to use such water to cool coke as it came out of their ovens. The result was that many of these same toxic agents were vaporized and became part of the air breathed by workers and the local communities.

‡ In Studying for an Exam, if you are scared by all you have to do and this interferes with getting started, consider "chunking." This involves setting aside l0% or even less of what you have to do, and

treating it as your immediate target. When this much is done, increase the percentage and repeat the exercise. Having made a start, which for many is the most difficult thing to do, you will not only feel more relaxed but your own momentum is likely to carry you beyond your original target. You're now on your way. If this sounds like a recipe for fooling yourself, it is because that is exactly what it is. But it's all in a good cause.

Everyone seems to be against pollution, and we know what causes most of it. So why is there still so much pollution taking place? The writer and social activist, Jim Hightower, suggests the answer in his account of what happened when the Royal Caribbean Cruise Lines were caught recently dumping its garbage in the ocean. To show up in court on their behalf, they hired "two former heads of the U.S. Department of Justice Environmental Crimes Section, two former U.S. Attorneys General, two former federal prosecutors, a handful of former Government officials, a law professor, and (count them) four retired admirals. Then they spent a fortune painting themselves green: buying ads during the Super Bowl...hiring ex-Environmental Protection Agency officials to be on their board, and writing large checks to environmental groups." (*Lowdown*, March, 2000) If this is what a corporation does when it gets caught, what do you think it does not to get caught, starting with securing laws that allow it to do what it wishes in the first place?

Meanwhile the problems connected with the diminishing supply of fresh air and fresh water, deforestation, the growing hole in the ozone layer, shrinking polar ice caps, rising sea level, desertification, global warming, vanishing species and increasingly erratic weather conditions get progressively worse. Caring for nature, it seems, costs too much money, cutting into the profits of companies whose only concern is with making profits.

Latest news from the ecological war zone: Just today (December 12, 2000), the *New York Times* reports that even the more modest increase in temperature predicted by some scientists would reduce the

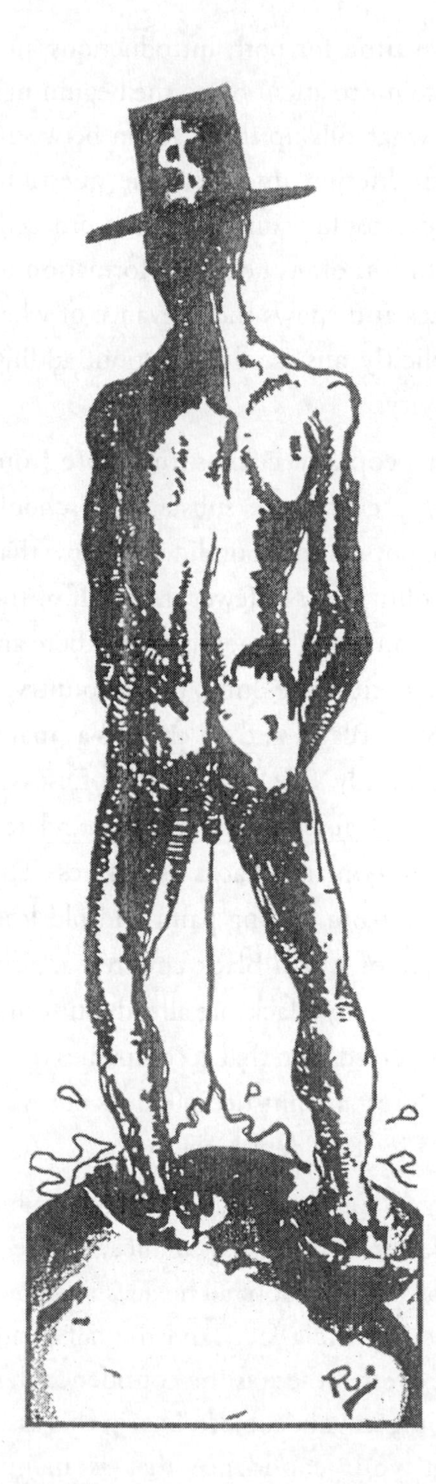

world's rice harvest by 20-40% by 2100. The larger increase forecast by other scientists would reduce rice production down to almost zero in the same period. Rice, of course, is a staple food for about two-thirds of the world's population.The clock is ticking for this poor planet of our's. Can you hear it?

Hey, stop fouling our nest!
Or else...

Old Kenyan proverb:
"Treat the earth well. It was not given to you by your parents, but loaned to you by your children."

‡ In Essay Exams, be sure to leave time for both introductions and conclusions. Most teachers devote more attention to the beginnings and endings of answers than to what fills up the space in between. Generally speaking, a good introduction interprets the question, defines a key term or two, and indicates how one is going to proceed. Generally speaking, a good conclusion offers no new information or arguments but simply summarizes and shows the relevance of what came before. It should also explicitly answer the question, adding whatever qualifications are necessary.

You already know, of course, that people of color suffer more from unemployment, slum housing, poor medical care, substandard schools and urban violence than the general population, but did you know that they are also the main victims of pollution? No fewer than half of the Blacks and Hispanics in the U.S. live in neighborhoods where there are hazardous waste dumps. The largest toxic waste dump in the country is in Emelle, Alabama, a city that is 80% Black, and no city has as many toxic dumps as Chicago's predominantly Black south side. Diseases caused by pollution are similarly mal-distributed. Pollution related asthma, for example, hits five times as many Blacks as Whites. The danger of lead poisoning that comes from pealing paint and old lead pipes is particularly acute, with 44% of urban Black children at risk. Eight million children, mostly poor, mostly Black, are already suffering from lead poisoning and the mental retardation that accompanies it.

The Talmud says, "Who can protest an injustice and does not is an accomplice in the act." Tell that to Vice President Lieberman.

‡ What role does confidence play in producing good exam results? There is, of course, the confidence based on ignorance, where a student knows so little that he has no clue about all he doesn't know. The Bible speaks of this as "pride before a fall," and the fall (read: "fail") is certain. On the other extreme, there is the confidence that comes from being perfectly at home in your subject, but, in this case, it is what you know and not your confidence that is mainly

responsible for your good grade. In between, which I take to be the typical case, where you know a good deal about the subject but nowhere near enough, confidence that you can ace the exam contributes to the clarity and forcefulness with which you express your views and becomes an important factor in your success.

By giving you exam tactics that work, by letting you peek into the minds of teachers as they make up and grade exams, and by explaining how the entire exam situation fits into the life processes of our capitalist society, my aim has been to increase your self-confidence, to give you that warm feeling that you are now ready—well—to take exams and remake the world.

Am I being objective? To the extent that "objective" means neutral, clearly not. But it is impossible to be neutral on the big social and political questions of the day, and those who claim to be are either unaware of the relation of their values to what they say, how they say it and what they emphasize, and even what they choose to study, or they are lying. To the extent that "objective" means being honest, open to hearing other points of view, and fair with those who disagree with me, then I claim to be more objective than most of my colleagues, who often use the term "objective" to hide their lack of neutrality.

Am I being objective? To the extent that "objective" means dry and unemotional, again the answer is "no." But how can one remain unmoved by the horrors, mostly unnecessary, mostly correctable, with which we are surrounded? Yet, misled by an overly restrictive notion of "objective," most professors try to do just that. What the American novelist, Jack London, said about our universities in 1906, unfortunately, still applies: "I found the university...clean and noble, but I did not find the university alive. I found the American university had this ideal as phrased by a professor from the University of Chicago: 'The passionless pursuit of passionless intelligence'—clean and noble, I grant you, but not alive enough...And in the reflection of this university ideal I find the conservatism and unconcern of the American people toward those who are suffering, who are in want."

Should you be objective? Of course. But that shouldn't mean avoiding to take a strong position when the facts and arguments you've assembled call for it, or repressing the emotions they evoke, or refusing to act or urging others to act when doing so may make a difference.

‡ In True/False Exams, remember: If any part of a statement is false, the whole statement is false. Some teachers try to trick students by packing a statement with a lot of true information only to spoil it with a minor fact that is false. Watch out.

Student taking a True/False test is observed flipping a coin. "What are you doing?" asked the teacher. "I'm working out answers," he replies. At the end of the hour, the teacher notices that the student is flipping his coin furiously, and asks, "Now what are you doing?" "I'm checking my answers."

Societies all possess a set of rules for the game of life that their citizens are forced to play. In our society, the game is called "Capitalism." And, like any game, it identifies players, sets out a series of moves, determines what is meant by winning and losing, provides rewards and punishments, Chance Cards, and even a "currency"—real money—that players accumulate (or try to), which allows each one to see how well he's doing. All games are invented. Except where societies are concerned, those who invented the game are given the title of "Founding Fathers." If you look closely at the rules of the game of any society, you'll find them clearly biased in favor of the class or classes to which its Founding Fathers belonged. They just wanted to make sure that they and their kind kept on winning.

The rules of our Capitalist Game? They were nicely summarized by one of my students who said: "Our society seems to assume that the rich never have enough money, and that the poor always have too much." Which is how Henry Ford could say in the midst of the Great Depression, "These really are good times, but only a few know it."

Anybody ready for a new game?

‡ In Essay Exams, don't "dis" the teacher. We're a poorly paid lot, and all many teachers have going for them is the certainty (okay, so it's only a hope) that what they're doing deserves respect, at least from their students. So when you disagree with what a teacher has said in class, do so in a way that doesn't leave him/her feeling like a blithering idiot, or feeling that you think he/she is one. Thus, in introducing what the teacher said or what you know him/her to believe, it is best to begin by admitting what part of it is true, under what special conditions it applies, or why someone might believe it, before offering your criticism and finally your own views.

In general, it is wise to take cognizance of other people's views, to the extent that you know them, before presenting your own. This way, at least, you have a better chance that they will read or listen to you without "putting their tongue in their ear" (old Chinese expression for missing what another is saying because one is too busy preparing a reply).

The last exam hint is to be handled carefully, because one of the deadliest poisons produced by our educational system at all levels is *respect.* I have no quarrel with respecting someone who has a batting average of .300, or who excels as a ballet dancer or physicist, or who is a dedicated teacher. What I object to is the respect that is demanded of us because of whom the person is, because of the superior position he or she holds in one of the hierarchies to which we belong—school, work, state, church and even family—rather than because of what that person has done. This is simply an underhanded way to get us to put our reason and judgement aside and to accept the legitimacy of the hierarchy as such as well as the purpose it serves, and even to grant automatic approval to whatever it does. Those who encourage us to develop this kind of respect know this, which is reason enough not to respect them and to begin to look more critically at the various hierarchies they represent.

‡ In Multiple Choice Exams, the longest answer is frequently the correct one, because its very length can be a sign that the teacher has tried to avoid ambiguity. It would be unusually perverse to dress a fiction up in much more flowery attire than the facts...but then you know your teacher much better than Ido.

Real intelligence often shows more clearly in the kind of questions one asks than in the answers one gives. Few things impress me about someone as much as the quality of his/her questions. The educator, Neil Postman, considers question asking the basis of all knowledge and our most important educational tool. Unfortunately, for most people curiosity generally peaks between the ages of four to six. This is not because after that they know all the answers, but because in most cases their questions have not received the respectful hearing that they deserve. It is important, however, that you don't give up, that you continue to ask questions of everyone (and especially of yourself), and that you persist until your world "makes sense." This comment can double as an exam hint: good essay answers can be organized around a series of related questions and can even end with a question, a new and, hopefully, more important question raised by the answer you provided.

Because questions often have a harder bite than answers, I also believe that the radical movement would be much further along if its members wrote fewer leaflets with answers to questions that people are not yet asking and spent more time just adding question marks to the mind numbing slogans that surround us on all sides: "Vote for Gore?" "Jesus Saves?" "You Can Count on Geritol?" Get the idea?

A WORKER READS HISTORY

by Bertolt Brecht

Who built the seven gates of Thebes?
The books are filled with names of kings.
Was it kings who hauled the craggy blocks of stone?
And Babylon, so many times destroyed,
Who built the city up each time? ...

Caesar beat the Gauls.
Was there not even a cook in his army?
Philip of Spain wept as his fleet
Was sunk and destroyed. Were there no other tears?
Frederick the Great triumphed in the Seven Years War. Who
Triumphed with him?

Each page a victory,
At whose expense the victory ball?
Every ten years a great man,
Who paid the piper?

So many particulars. So many questions.

FIVE

Ramsay MacDonald, one-time leader of the British Labour Party, posed the question: If men were free but their hands belonged to a class of masters, would they really be free? His answer was "No," because people need their hands in order to work and live. Well, our hands belong to us, but—as MacDonald points out—all the machines, factories, office buildings and raw materials we use in our work, in sum everything we need in order to do the tasks that enable us to live, belong to someone else. These necessary extensions of our hands, without which we can do little more than scratch ourselves, belong to another class of masters, though we don't call them that. So, are we really free?

‡ In Essay and Oral Exams, how careful must one be in qualifying one's conclusions? Very careful. A common error is for students to offer evidence or arguments that support a conclusion limited as to number, kind, time or area, but to make it seem that it applies to everyone, everywhere, always. Also, when your conclusion is—and can only be—tentative, likely or uncertain, say so. Also, it may sometimes be the case that you can't come to a conclusion, or that there are two possible conclusions. If this is what the "facts" call for, say so explicitly. Assuming the facts justify it, carefully qualified conclusions usually go over very big with examiners.

Counterfeit money and counterfeit words have a lot in common. Both seem to be what they are not, and neither really delivers, value in one case, sense in the other; but they often fool people, and, of course, they are produced with this in mind. While not very serious if it is a matter of $1 and $5 bills, it becomes immensely more so when the denominations reach $100 and $1,000. The same is true of words.

"Freedom" is a $1,000,000 word, and the one in general circulation today is counterfeit. It doesn't enable us to understand the full sense of what it points to. As most people in the U.S. use "freedom," it means the absence of restraints. That is, if no one is holding a gun to your head and there are no bars in front of your face, you are said to be free, which makes the poorest bum in the park as free as the richest capitalist. The fact that some people possess the means to take advantage of not being restrained to do what they want, and others don't, makes freedom in the case of the latter a cruel joke or worse. Freedom to be left alone to starve, to freeze, to remain ignorant can't really be freedom. For freedom to be worthy of the sacrifices made in its name, it must include something of the real life conditions that enable people to do what they want as well as the fact that no one is actively keeping them from doing it. But let's not forget the counterfeit term, if only to learn who benefits from this deception and how they have managed to fool us for so long.

Here is a good place to start: Dick Armey, a G.O.P. Congressman from Texas, advised his fellow Republican lawmakers, "No matter what cause you advocate, you must sell it in the language of freedom."

‡ On Factual Exams, another aid to guessing is suggested by the fact that teachers who offer several possibilities, as in "Choose between A, B, C, and D," like to spread the correct answer around a bit. So, if most of the answers you know to be correct, fall under A and B, it is very likely that most of the answers you are not sure of fall under C and D.

"The law in all its majesty forbids rich and poor alike from sleeping under bridges and stealing bread." It is over one hundred years since the French novelist, Anatole France, penned these words, and we are still waiting for the first rich person to be arrested for sleeping under a bridge or stealing bread. Apparently, economic inequality is enough to render most forms of legal equality null and void. Worse, whenever people suffering from unequal conditions are given formal equality, i.e., possess the same legal rights and duties, the result is generally a worsening of real inequality, because those who are favored by conditions will use the level playing field to increase their already sizeable advantages.

Our capitalist society is without a peer in giving out legal rights with one hand and taking them back with the other. For example, each of us has the right to say what he or she wants; it's called "freedom of speech." It's just hard, without the kind of money to buy space in the major media, to get others to hear what you have to say. "Sure the press is free," as one of our guys put it, "for those who can afford to own one."

An alternative approach to rights is offered by the early 20th century American humorist, Mr. Dooley, who says, "Don't ask for rights. Take them. And don't let anyone give them to you. A right that is handed to you for nothing has something wrong with it. It's more likely a wrong turned inside out."

‡ In an Essay Exam, if you can give two versions of the answer, what two different thinkers or schools have written on this subject, so much the better. This is considered a sophisticated answer.

Spying, at least inside the U.S., is something only foreigners do, right? Wrong. Americans are spied on legally and illegally by a host of federal, state and local agencies. In the 1960's, for example, the Chicago Police Dept. admitted to having secret dossiers on 117,000 local citizens, 141,000 out-of-towners and 14,000 organizations. No one knows how much of this is still going on.

Have you put in a request for your F.B.I. file yet (something you have a legal right to see)? I haven't broken any law, but my 100 page file placed me in cities where I have never been, indicated that my wife and I had been followed in Milwaukee (on a visit to my parents) when we went to a store to buy milk for our baby, and quoted an unnamed informer who said, "Ollman is a communist just like his sister." I have no sister, and I wasn't a communist—then. I was also constantly referred to in the report as "BERTELL OLLMAN a.k.a. BERTEL OLLMAN" (pretty clever of me to operate with a pseudonym that no one would recognize). Unfortunately, stupidity never made any cop less dangerous.

‡ There used to be a time, I'm told, when exams were mainly used to serve the needs of teaching (as a means of helping students learn), and, no doubt, here and there this still occurs. More and more, however, this relationship has been turned around, so that today most teaching is exam driven (has become a means to help students pass their exams). Here, it is not so much what one has learned that is important, but the evidence—the exam and, especially, the grade received—that one has learned it. In the process, most professors function more (or more often) as exam coaches and trainers than as teachers. (With this book, of course, I have accepted to march in step with my peers, but only so I can alert you as to what is happening, and to explore whether together we can find a better way.)

The key to understanding this turn-around is to see that exams play a role in the world of work as well as in the world of education, and to those who have power over both the first is far more important. While most of education is aimed at giving you the knowledge, skills and attitudes toward work and hierarchy required by your future—probably corporate—employer, exams (and the grades received in them) cap this process by helping your employer match the individual to the job. Exam results inform him much better, he believes, than you can (or would) as to what you can do and how well you can do it.

Before the spread of higher education in our country, whatever training, socialization and sorting out of its work force a company required, it had to do on its own and at its own expense. Now universities and colleges perform these functions; they have become a combination of training centers, finishing schools, employment agencies and warehouses for temporarily unneeded workers—all at public (meaning "non-corporate") expense. In the process, education in America (and the other capitalist countries are quickly following suit) has become an extension of work, and of the needs and interests—social and political as well as technological and organizational—of those who control our work. To ensure that all this runs smoothly, the ruling class itself, together with a few of its more trusted hirelings, occupies the commanding heights of the educational system. Do you recall the question I raised earlier about why the boards of trustees of most of our universities are dominated by big businessman and their lawyers? Well, here's one mystery solved.

"Free enterprise," this is where the enterprises with power, which comes from the amount of wealth they control, are free to use it as they wish against workers, consumers and small business-people alike. "Free trade" is when the strongest enterprises are given a green light to clobber their weaker foreign competitors as well. Businesses and our business oriented Government are for trade unbounded by political restrictions whenever it benefits them, and against it when it doesn't. Brazil has recently complained that the U.S. Government is interfering in one way or another with the export of over eighty different items from that country, all the while extolling the virtues of free trade. The truth is that no one actually believes in the "principle" of free trade, except, perhaps, a few of my more naive colleagues in the academy.

"Free market" refers to a system in which everyone has a choice to buy and sell whatever they want (including labor power) at a price they find acceptable. On this model, people have no one to blame but themselves and the bad choices they've made for the outcomes they don't like. But can poor people choose to buy goods they can't afford? Or can workers choose to sell their labor power for a decent wage to employers who don't want it or are only willing to pay half that amount to get it? Rather than focusing on the moment of choice, it is the unequal conditions in which people make their choices and which narrowly prescribe what can be chosen that should get our attention. Only then can the free market be seen for what it really is: a way for the strong to obtain what they want from the weak by ignoring—and fooling the weak to ignore—the conditions that underlie the vast disparities in their power.

"Okay," I can hear some readers thinking, "the free market may be unfair, unjust, undemocratic and even unfree, but isn't it economically more efficient than a planned economy?" The answer is: only if you leave out all the expenses associated with advertising, undermining the health of millions of workers and consumers and polluting the environment, all of which are treated as "external" costs under present arrangements. Beyond this, there is the enormous waste occasioned by allowing a large portion of the machine, raw materials, and workers available to go unused when using them would not bring a sufficient profit to the owners. Those who praise our capitalist market economy for its efficiency—focusing on how hard people work when threatened by the wolf of material deprivation at the door (a mixed blessing at best)—never take all this unnecessary waste and expense into account.

‡ In Oral Exams, if you don't know something, don't try to fake it. This is the path to perdition. Your professors are likely to recognize what you are doing and ask more questions on this same point. The result is that something that should have taken no more than a minute has now occupied an important chunk of the exam and become a major element in their evaluation of your performance. On the other hand, if you think you know the answer but are not sure of it, don't hesitate to give it, adding only that you are uncertain.

It is very common for university students to think that practically everyone else is brainwashed by advertising but that they're not. Forget it. We all are, and more than we realize. How could it be otherwise? American businesses spend over a *trillion* dollars a year (that's about 1/6 of the Gross Domestic Product) on advertising and public relations. These industries employ 150,000 people, which is about 20,000 more than the number of reporters in the country, and produce or influence about 40% of everything we see, read and hear. Most of what you're wearing and eating and planning to do this weekend—to say nothing of your political predilections—is evidence for how well this spinning and smiling and downright lying has done its job.

To counter all this advertising we would need to have a lot of information that even in this "age of information" is not readily available. The Canadian philosopher, John McMurtry, points out that "what is genetically modified or not, what bears criminally exploited labor or not, what is pollutive in its manufacture and distribution or not, what destroys species and fellow mammals or not, what is carcinogenic or not, what pays profits to genocidal regimes or not" are all things we are prohibited from learning by new trade laws that consider such information as "discrimination against the process of production." In sum, the capitalists don't want you to have the facts you need to make informed choices as a consumer. Nor is it easy, given capitalist control of the media, to acquire the information we need to make informed choices as voters and citizens. If mainstream talk is all about freedom of choice, reality presents a picture of thorough-going manipulation with advertising, public relations, news broadcasts, entertainment and—dare I say it?—"education" as the key manipulators.

Hegel declared that "freedom is the recognition of necessity," by which he meant that it is only *after* taking into account all the ways in which what we do is determined by forces outside our control that we can begin to exercise any real freedom in choosing what to do. (To this, Marx would add—and to take control, eventually, of the very forces that have until now controlled us.)

‡ In Essay Exams, pay careful attention to the key verb that instructs you on what to do. "Discuss," for example, allows more leeway and offers more opportunities for embroidery than "compare," which, in turn, is more open ended than "explain" or "evaluate." Try to become sensitive to the nuances of meaning that set these verbs apart from one another and from other verbs that occasionally take their place: "trace," "describe," "defend," "criticize," etc. A lot of the irrelevance I warned against earlier is the result of flattening out the differences between these verbs. Note, too, that you are never asked to say all that you know about a subject, so be sure that your answer doesn't make it appear this is what you are doing.

As Jesse Jackson points out, "Poor folks steal, rich folks embezzle...poor folks lie, rich folks prevaricate." A century ago, the radical humorist, T-Bone Slim, also reminded us: "Only the poor break the laws—the rich evade them." Capitalist reality is disguised not only by specialized language (each academic discipline has one), legal language, bureaucratic language and just plain unintelligible jargon, but also by euphemisms (Jackson's examples), treating what is dead as if it were alive ("The market is tired") and heavy use of passive constructions ("Benefits are being reduced"), which keep people from seeing who has done it and what the alternatives might have been. The Pentagon, for whom civilian casualties have become "collateral damage," is but the most obvious offender and therefore less dangerous than the rest of the Establishment, whose linguistic manipulations are more difficult to recognize.

The degree to which this manipulation is conscious was revealed recently by a booklet entitled, "Language: A Key Mechanism of Control," given to Republican candidates for office by GOPAC, a conservative political action committee headed by Newt Gingrich, then Speaker of the U.S. House of Representatives. In it, candidates are told that when speaking of themselves they should use words like "environment, peace, freedom, fair, flag, we-us-our family and humane." While the expressions they were encouraged to use when speaking of their opponents were: "betray, sick, pathetic, lie, liberal, hypocrisy, permissive attitude and self-serving."

With verbal traps waiting for us at every turn, the struggle to make sense of the world demands our constant attention, a keen, critical outlook that takes nothing for granted, the courage to question authority, and just enough anger at being fooled so often to make it all come together.

‡ Just how biased can tests be? Well, in 1912, Henry Goddard, a distinguished psychologist, administered what he claimed were "culture free" I.Q. tests to new immigrants on Ellis Island, and found that 83% of Jews, 80% of Hungarians, 79% of Italians, and 87% of Russians were "feebleminded," adding that "all feebleminded are at least potential criminals."

Yes, I.Q. tests have gotten a little better since then, but you can still find the following: "Q.: What is the essential difference between work and play? High I.Q. answer: Work is energy used for something useful and play is just wasted energy. Low I.Q. answer: You'd rather play than work." Or, here's another: "Q.: Why do we elect (or need to have) Senators and Congressmen? High I.Q. answer: Electing Senators makes Government responsible to the people. Low I.Q.

answer: Senators help control people in the U.S." I guess I have a very low I.Q.

While it is unlikely that most of the tests you take are so slanted, neither should you assume that all biases have been removed or even could be removed, given the character of the testing process, the attitudes of those who make up the test and who correct it, and the variety of people—coming from so many different backgrounds—who take it.

Life Exam Question: Consider the last few exams that you've taken; from what biases, if any, did you suffer?

'YOU KIDS NOWADAYS ARE SO LUCKY—
WE NEVER HAD LIBERAL EDUCATIONS BACK WHEN I WAS A BOY!'

SIX

Boss to employee: "Young man, you have risen very fast in this company. Two years ago you began as an office boy; in a couple months you were a clerk; then you became a salesman, after that assistant manager, then manager. Now you are the vice president of the company. What have you to say about all this?"
Employee: "Thanks, Dad."

‡ This book is trying to help you do better on exams. Should you wish to do worse, *The Art of Pluck* (1835), written by an Oxford University student, Scriblerus Redivivus (e.k.a, Edward Caswell), offers advice on how to fail exams, with chapters on various forms of "idleness": smoking, love, billiards, novels, rowing and drinking. Yes, I also thought that was a pretty thin list. Why don't you fill it out by writing down all the things you think you shouldn't be doing if you want to do better on exams. Don't be too hard on yourself, but don't be too easy either.

In John Guare's play, "Marco Polo Sings a Solo," a transvestite has herself impregnated with a sperm she had deposited in a sperm bank when she was a male, and has a baby to whom she is both mother and father. One person on his/her own doing it all! Here we have capitalism's ideal for solving every problem. Forget cooperation and collective effort. Let the sheriff do it. Hence, the public's fascination for super-heros and equally super-villains, who between them account for everything important that happens.

INDIVIDUALISM (the theory)

It's a nice children's story, except that it is told to adults as well as to children. The underlying message is that every individual can get what he/she wants—without the help of others—through a little imagination and a lot of hard work; consequently, that those who have already gotten what they want must have done just this; and, therefore, that they deserve what they've got. While not wishing to disparage either imagination or hard work, the question you have to answer is: Can a transvestite really impregnate herself and have a baby with one of her own sperm? Or, when can a little cooperation help?

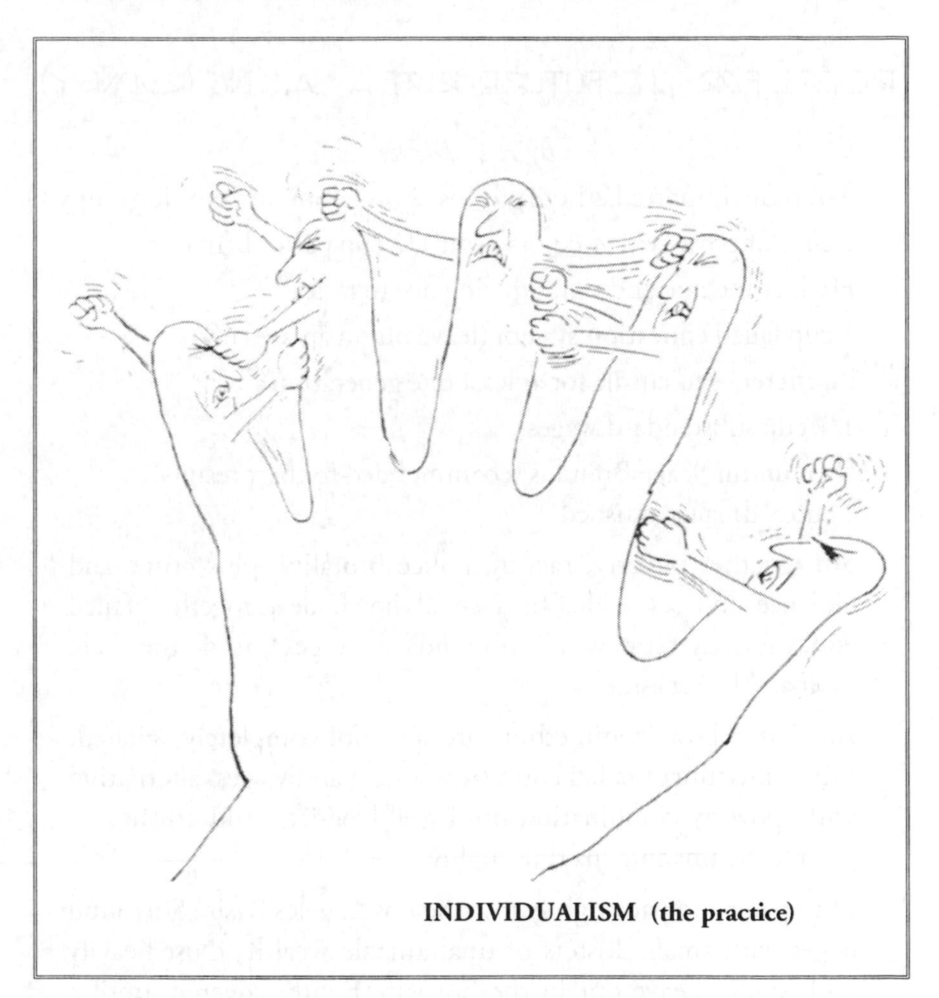

INDIVIDUALISM (the practice)

‡ In all Written Exams, block out your time at the start so you know roughly how long to spend on each section of the exam and, if possible, on each question. This does not mean you will spend the same amount of time on every question, or that you should, but simply that you now have a standard for judging when is "enough." In Factual Exams, harder questions may take a little more time and easy questions a little less, but that's okay, unless most questions turn out to be hard ones. In Essay Exams, your best answers are likely to take a little more time, but that's okay too—given you don't overdo it—since it is your best and worst answers that the teacher is most likely to remember when he or she picks up the grading pencil.

RECIPE FOR THE FUTURE: RIOT Á LA KING (RODNEY)

by R.F. Meyer

6 or more imported ethnic groups; 2 or 3 domestic ethnic groups
2 cups of poverty; 1/4 cup racism; 1/2 cup police brutality
High crime rate and random violence to taste.
1 cup failed education system (leave out in an area of indifference to curdle for at least one generation)
1/2 cup substandard wages
(Minimum Wage Brand is recommended for best results)
1 cup of dreams, crushed

Sift together poverty, racism, police brutality, plus crime and violence and set aside. In a small bowl, beat together failed education system with substandard wages until they are inseparable. Set aside.

In a larger bowl, whip ethnic groups until completely agitated. Stir in mixture of failed education system and wages, alternating with poverty combination until well blended. Add crushed or ground dreams and mix thoroughly.

Dump out and pack tightly into the Los Angeles Basin. Surround edges with small clusters of unattainable wealth. Dust heavily with smog. Leave out in the hot sun, tightly covered, until a sudden increase in anger, frustration and resentment, triggered by an obvious failure of the justice system, causes it to boil over.

Serves any number of journalists and media pundits. Recommended wine is vintage 1965 Watts.

Note: This recipe can be adapted for any city. Leftovers keep well.

‡ In Practical Exams (experiments and controlled exercises), "lay out all your tools and materials at the start. Be sure you know where everything you might need is and that it is all available in the right amount." As if you didn't know. Or, if you didn't, you shouldn't be allowed to walk the streets by yourself, let alone take exams. I only

include these points to remind you what typical exam advice is like. Most instruction about our government and economic system is equally innocuous, which are two good reasons you need this book.

Alexis de Tocqueville, a young French aristocrat traveling around the United States in the 1830s, witnessed American Indians driven out of their homes in the middle of winter. The old, the very young, the sick were left to die in the snow. What shocked de Tocqueville the most is that our pioneers could kill human beings without, in their own eyes, "violating a single great principle of morality." It would be impossible, he thought, to find other examples of such wanton destruction which outwardly displayed "more respect for the laws of humanity."

A decade later, the United States helped itself to a third of Mexico in a war that a later president, Ulysses S. Grant, described as the most unjust war that a strong country had ever conducted against a weak one. The ideological rationalization of this action spoke of our "manifest destiny." In 1898, we started a war with Spain in order to add Cuba and the Philippines to the growing American empire, though the reason given at the time was to help these countries win their independence. In our more recent history, as Noam Chomsky, who draws together these threads, points out, "the war against Vietnam left maybe three or four million dead and three countries ruined." Yet, from Ronald Reagan to the Public Broadcasting System (PBS) the war was presented as a noble cause, or at worse a tactical mistake. Like our pioneer ancestors, we destroyed these countries with the "greatest respect for the laws of humanity."

In 1990, our Government used the most sophisticated weaponry in the world to kill hundreds of thousands of Iraquis in order—so it was said—to give the medieval monarchy of Kuwait back its freedom. In 1998, it was Yugoslavia's turn to be bombed into submission for mistreating some of its own subjects. And even now our dollars and "military advisers" are aiding the fascistic armies of Peru and Columbia (and, until just yesterday, Nicaragua, Guatemala, El Salvador,

Indonesia, Chile and Brazil) to murder, torture and make disappear countless thousands of their own people to protect what we insist on calling their democracies. Apparently, when America's allies and dependents engage in actions that are far worse than what the Serbs were accused of doing to the Kosovars this does not amount to mistreating their own subjects.

In his book, *Mein Kampf*, Hitler introduced us to the theory of the Big Lie. Everyone, he said, tells little lies, so they have no trouble recognizing them when they hear them. But few people have the audacity to tell truly Big Lies, nor enough cynicism to believe that others might. Consequently, one has a better chance of getting away with a truly Big Lie than a small one. Hitler was not alone in applying this lesson. One of the biggest and, perhaps for that reason, most successful lies in all of history is that the foreign policy of the United States Government has been directed to protecting human rights, extending democracy and defending freedom. But if these are not the aims of our rulers, what are they? What could possibly justify the grisly historical record?

An authoritative reply to these questions was offered by General Smedley Butler of the U.S. Marines at an American Legion Convention back in 1931, when he said, "I was a gangster for Wall Street: I helped make Mexico and especially Tampico safe for American oil interests in 1914; I helped make Haiti and Cuba a decent place for the National City Bank boys to collect revenue in; I helped purify Nicaragua for the International banking house of Brown Brothers in 1909-12; I brought light to the Dominican Republic for American sugar interests in 1916; and I helped make Honduras 'right' for American fruit companies in 1903." This startling confession should help us understand what really motivates American foreign policy, always has (and will, if we allow it).

An English reporter once asked Mahatma Ghandi what he thought of Western Civilization. Gandi answered, "I think it would be a good idea."

NEW WORLD ORDERS
A NEW ERA OF PEACE AND PROSPERITY THROUGH-OUT THE WORLD, HOLD THE SKEPTICISM!
A NEW AWARENESS OF THE SPECIAL PROBLEMS OF THE THIRD WORLD, AND A SIDE OF BALONEY!
A NEW SENSITIVITY TO THE ECOLOGICAL CONSEQUENCES OF THE HEADLONG PURSUIT OF PROFIT, ON A BED OF PUBLIC RELATIONS!
MStevens

‡ In Oral Exams, there is never enough time for professors to ask all their questions. Consequently, they may break into your answer before you have finished in order to get onto their next question. Usually this is a sign that you have said enough and not that they're dissatisfied, so this shouldn't bother you. However, it does mean that the brilliant conclusion that you've left for last will never be heard. So try to get to your main point(s) as quickly as possible, leaving most examples, qualifications, implications, and the like for later, if there is time. This suggestion applies to Oral Exams only.

WHAT DID YOU LEARN IN SCHOOL TODAY?

song by Tom Paxton

What did you learn in school today dear little boy of mine?

I learned that Washington never told a lie
I learned that soldiers seldom die, I learned that everybody's free
That's what the teacher said to me
And that's what I learned in school today, That's what I learned in school...

What did you learn in school today dear little boy of mine?...
I learned that policemen are my friends
I learned that justice never ends
I learned that murderers die for their crimes even if we make a mistake sometimes
And that's what I learned in school today, That's what I learned in school...

I learned our government must be strong
It's always right and never wrong
Our leaders are the finest men and we elect them again and again
And that's what I learned in school today, That's what I learned in school...

‡ In Studying for an exam, you should spend as little time as possible reading new material, but this assumes that you have already read all you were supposed to and I know this is seldom the case. Hence, there is generally a trade-off to make between getting a better grip on what you already know (sort of) and learning new material. If what you haven't read is less than a third of what you should have read, my advice is to devote most of your time to review, especially for Essay and Oral Exams, where there is generally a choice of questions and it is very important that you answer at least a few questions very well. In the case of Factual Exams, however, I would give a higher priority to finishing the reading you haven't done, since you can't possibly know facts that you never encountered. It is better by far, of course, to keep up with the reading, and not be caught in such a fix.

To talk about the Third World's "debt" or "balance of payments" problem rather than their imperialist exploitation problem is to take for granted the capitalists' point of view. It is like Southern racists talking about their "Black problem," or Hitler referring to his "Jewish problem."

The same thing happens in talk of the "national debt." "Debt" suggests that one has a moral as well as a legal duty to repay. But why should the large majority of Americans repay the few rich who got *their* government to spend *our* money (and then some) serving *their* interests while making profits for *their* corporations? A more accurate term for these trillions that they want to squeeze out of us through additional taxes and reduced services is "tribute," which is what rulers have always exacted from those over whom they reign. The truth is that our capitalist ruling class forces the people under their sway, in the U.S. and abroad, to pay them "tribute," and then adds insult to injury by trying to fool us into viewing it as our "debt."

‡ Make-up Exams, because they're taken after the scheduled exam, you have more time to study for them. That's a plus. Knowing this, many teachers are likely to make them more difficult than regular exams

and to be more strict in grading them. That's a big minus. It doesn't endear you to the teacher either that make-ups often involve him/her in extra work. Thus, make-up exams are to be avoided if possible.

A recent poll asked voters which are the areas in which the Government spends the most money. About half of them answered foreign aid and welfare, each of which takes up about 1% of the budget. Even more people are probably unaware that 70% of foreign aid is spent in the U.S., providing jobs and profits for Americans, or that many welfare recipients also have jobs, but that these don't pay enough to live on. But the real problem seems to be with the labels, which suggests that some folks are getting something for nothing, so a little bit is blown up to appear like much more than it really is. Solution: let's change the names. From now on we'll call foreign aid "export promotion" and "bail outs," and we'll call welfare "price supports" and "research grants." This will allow those who really need help to get the far greater sums that corporations are now getting under these labels, and those in the public whose main complaint is with the terms "aid" and "welfare" will be appeased.

An alternative is to call what corporations are now getting under these various labels by its proper name, which is "welfare" (more than $125 billion a year from the national government alone, according to *Time Magazine*), and then sharing the money that goes to welfare more equitably among all the people who qualify for it.

‡ In Essay Exams, try not to write very big. About half of the really bad papers I correct are written in very large letters. The connection is so close that I've tended to associate very large handwriting with poor and/or sloppy thinking. If it happens to me, I suspect it also happens to other teachers. Conclusion: if you have something to say, don't signal otherwise by writing too big. And if you don't have much to say, don't advertise it in this way. Also, don't doodle (yes, some students do) or leave too many ink blotches on your exam. They affect teachers in the same way.

The Kwegu and the Mursi are two tribes in Ethiopia that are involved in an unusual living arrangement. The Kwegu are the craftsmen; they build canoes, make axes, fix guns, etc. They also paddle the canoes across the swift rivers that are full of crocodiles, and they collect honey. The Mursi are farmers and herdsmen. In order to get married, a Kwegu male must give a cow as dowry to the family of his bride. This cow is provided by his Mursi patron for whom he is then obliged to do the different kinds of work mentioned above. The Kwegu, who are also discriminated against in various ways, obviously get the worse side of this bargain. Yet, they are convinced that they get as good as they give, because they believe that without the Mursi gift of a cow they couldn't pay the expected dowry. They simply can't conceive of getting married without a cow, or acquiring a cow by any other means than having the Mursi give them one. If they could, they wouldn't need the Mursi, and wouldn't accept to do all the work they do for them.

What, then, keeps the Kwegu from recognizing what all of us, I trust, would take as pretty obvious? There is, of course, the threat of force, of throwing "trouble-makers" into the crocodile infested rivers, but, over-all, the belief in the fairness of their exchange seems genuine. At the level of ideas, it appears that the Kwegu are trapped in their subservient role because they confuse and conflate historically conditioned circumstances—their need for cows in order to marry and the fact only the Mursi can provide them—with a natural function, the wish to mate.

There is a close parallel between the situation of the Kwegu and that of the workers in capitalist society. In our society, most workers have work only when capitalists, who own the means of production, distribution and exchange, hire them. As a result, many workers believe that without capitalists there would be no work. But working, or transforming nature to satisfy human needs, is a natural function of our species. It exists wherever there are people and is necessary to our collective survival. In this, it is like the Kwegu's need to mate. While allowing capitalists, who are only concerned with maximizing their profits, to determine who can use the machines and factories that are needed in order to work is the peculiar form that work takes in our period. It is like the Mursi providing the Kwegu with the cows the latter need to marry. Unfortunately, by focusing on the moment when the capitalist hires the worker, it would appear that the capitalists are as essential for any production to go on as the workers themselves. They even appear to be doing the workers a favor in hiring them for jobs. But as with the Kwegu and the Mursi, what has to happen for life to go on in any society has been confused with the *particular* way it goes on in our society. Need I add to whose benefit this works?

People will only strive to remove the capitalist straitjacket that impedes all their movements when they can clearly distinguish what comes from capitalism from what comes from the human condition, and grasp as part of this that things have been and may yet be otherwise. Our battlecry? "Kwegu of the world unite. You have nothing to lose but your Mursi."

‡ One of history's first exams is recorded in the ancient Greek philosopher Xenophon's essay, "The Education of Cyrus." Cyrus, then about ten years old, was soon to become a famous king of Persia. Cyrus' teacher presented him with the following problem: suppose you have a cloak (what they wore in those days) that was too big for you, and an older boy came along who was wearing a cloak that was too small for him. What should you do? Where, the teacher asked, does justice lie in this case?

Probably thinking this was a no-brainer, Cyrus quickly replied, "Why, I would exchange cloaks with him, so that each of us had a cloak that fit." On hearing this answer, the teacher pulled out his lash (standard equipment for teachers in those days) and began to whip Cyrus with it. "Wrong," he hollered. "Your cloak belongs to you, and his cloak belongs to him. Each should keep what is his." The underlying message: Respect Private Property. The lash and the words together, repeated again and again, soon won the contest with common sense, as, indeed, they continue to do today, where more sophisticated ways of delivering the message have allowed teachers to ease up a bit on the lash.

Viewed in this way, the story of Cyrus' cloak becomes a kind of ur-exam, the paradigm for all future exams, where the main aim is not to find out what the student knows but to prepare him for life in his society in which private property and the hierarchical relations it both produces and requires constitute the core values.

SEVEN

Number of walls the size of the Vietnam Memorial it would take to list all the Vietnamese who died in that war:

69

Number of courses on the Vietnam War required for graduation from West Point:

0

"If my soldiers were to begin to reflect, not one of them would remain in the ranks." —Frederick the "Great" of Prussia.

‡ First Prize for the best exam of the decade goes to the architecture professor who asked his students to design a better electric chair. Everyone who completed the exam was then failed. Now here is an exam that really taught students something.

In North Adams, Mass., one small businessman expressed frustration that at sixty-five he was too old to go to Saudi Arabia to fight in the war against Iraq. "Let the wimps step aside," he said. "I'll go in their place." Mr. D'Amico called himself a "strong supporter of our stand in the Persian Gulf." But, when pressed, he acknowledged that he was unsure just what that stand was. "That's something I would like to know," he said. "What are we fighting about?" (*New York Times*, November 15, 1990)

ARMY MEDICAL EXAMINER: "At last a perfect soldier!"

When I was an undergraduate at the University of Wisconsin in the mid-1950's, the American Legion started a campaign against the university library for containing too many books that were critical of the "American way of life." Intrigued, I wrote to the Legion asking what they meant by this expression, and received a reply from their State Chairman for Americanism (yes, he exists), who said he really didn't know what the "American way of life" is, but of one thing I could be sure, and that is that he was ready to give his life for it. It seems there are always some people who are ready to kill and be killed, or send others off to the slaughtering house, without knowing why. These people are called "patriots."

‡ In Essay and Oral Exams, should you adopt the teacher's point of view on the subject? This is a tough one. It is my experience that it is more important to show you know what the teacher thinks than to share his/her views. The real danger is to make it appear that you didn't read the materials that present the teacher's position or didn't listen to what he/she had to say in its defense. So if you disagree with the teacher on an important matter, indicate briefly what his/her position is and why you disagree before going on to develop your own view. This should work with all but the most biased and insecure teachers. Okay, okay, so there are more than a few out there.

"Nationalism" is often defined as a love of one's country and people, but it is better understood as the contempt felt for neighboring countries and peoples, and a shared misunderstanding of one's origins. "Patriotism" is, largely, the way we speak about *our* nationalism. While "love of country" is the blind attachment many people feel for the empty symbols—flags, anthem, clichés, etc.—with which this emotion comes dressed. No patriot loves his fellow citizens, for too many of them pray in the wrong church, or come in the wrong color, or speak with the wrong accent.

Instead, patriotism offers a lumpy stew of ghosts and other fantasies for the human ties between real people that capitalist competition and the insecurities it generates makes impossible. It is also a sop thrown to our isolation and feelings of loneliness. By encouraging us to live vicariously all the successes of the very class that despoils us, patriotism also keeps us from developing the rational hostility toward this class that they deserve. And always and everywhere, patriotism is a blank check we give to our rulers to spend our blood as they wish.

"Patriotism is the last refuge of the scoundrel."—Samuel Johnson, 18th century English critic

"What is patriotism but the love of the good things we ate in our childhood?" —Lin Yutang, Chinese philosopher

That's probably the nicest thing that can be said of it.

‡ In Essay Exams, how should one deal with a half remembered answer? It's best, of course, to choose another question. But if that is not possible, you can try to interpret the question in a way that makes what you do recall central and what you can't less relevant. Together with this, you can try to pad your answer with related facts (for teachers who are most impressed by facts) and arguments (for the rest of us). In the latter case, "picking a fight" with the question could also involve attacking its assumptions or implications, or examining who might have asked such a question and why, or inquiring into the kind of evidence that is needed for coming up with any answer. If there is anything the least bit sophisticated in what you have to say, many teachers will grant you the right to sound a little outrageous. For this tactic to work, it also helps if you write well, giving the impression of an intelligent though opinionated student who has used the question in order to take a stand.

Capitalism operates a lot like Three Card Monte, where the pieces are moved around so fast that it is almost impossible to guess where the red card is. Who or what is responsible? This is capitalism's red card. Once one recognizes—and it's almost impossible not to—that our society is falling apart, it becomes essential to know where to put the blame. Only then can we fix it, really fix it.

There are six main possibilities: 1) nothing and no one is responsible (that is, the problems from which we suffer are the result of natural economic laws); 2) the material forms in which the problems present themselves are responsible (that is, cars and, according to Reagan, trees cause pollution; technology causes unemployment; and so on); 3) we, ourselves, are responsible, so that those who suffer most have only brought it upon themselves (doesn't Pogo say, "We have met the enemy and it is us"?); 4) some group you don't like very much anyway—the Blacks, or Jews, or Japanese, or (fill in)—are to blame, and this just serves as another reason for disliking them; 5) the political leader or party in power is responsible, since it seems they can do whatever they want and they aren't doing anything to help (except the other party did more or less the same thing when they had the chance); or 6) the class that runs the economy and uses their power to maximize their profits are responsible (this power is used directly, through decisions regarding investment, pricing and hiring, and indirectly, through getting the Government, which they control, to act on their behalf).

Well, these are the possibilities. Now you decide. Who or what is chiefly responsible for unsafe and poorly paid jobs, unemployment, pollution, lousy health care, slums, poor schools, yes—even the high crime rate—and on and on. While you may not be responsible for any of these problems, you are responsible for deciding who or what is. To yourself. To your family. To the rest of us. Even in Three Card Monte, if you know how the trick is done, it is not too hard to locate the red card—and win.

‡ What is the relation between receiving a good grade and being especially likeable? And what about the old red apple routine? Teachers are only normal, and I suppose it's only normal to think that people you like and those who are especially nice to you are more intelligent. But it's also only normal to disapprove of insincerity, and the backlash it generates can produce a terrible burn. So don't crowd your teacher, but don't shy away from him/her either. On this one, its probably best doing what comes naturally, on the assumption that you're probably pretty likeable just being yourself.

"A MARXIST-TURNED-CAPITALIST FINDS THE BOTTOM LINE TOO LOW"

(New York Times Op-Ed, March 24, 1979)

by Bertell Ollman

"Tote that barge, lift that bale, secure better finances, or lose that sale."

Old Man River is not what it used to be, and neither is sleep, food, health, fun, friendship or conversation. For I am now a businessman, a leaser if not yet owner of means of production, an employer of labor, a seller of commodities.

It was a year ago that a half dozen other socialist professors and I started a corporation to produce and market my Marxist board game, *Class Struggle*. What began as a chance to mix politics with fun and add to our pedagogical bag of tricks soon became a serious business and I, with it, a serious—if not too effective—businessman.

In the game business, four large companies determine pretty much what gets produced, distributed, advertised and, consequently, played with by the American people. Afraid of alienating conservative customers, the big four would not even consider our game. Our efforts to find an independent producer were a nightmare that only ended with our paying about twice what any large company would pay for a similar product. Bankers were endlessly amused when I offered them a chance to hedge their bets by financing a Marxist board game, but—with one small exception—they stuck to their rule of lending money only to businesses that can prove they don't really need it.

All this to arrive on the desk of store buyers who, as often as not, were more concerned with the color of the box (black is out) and the amount of shelf-space it would occupy than with the intrinsic qualities of the game. Outside New York, there was some rumbling about the game's "ideological character"—as if Monopoly were neutral—but with the help of over 150 media stories, the game was selling and selling out practically everywhere. How surprised everyone seemed to be that a Marxist could be funny! Some papers have reported that we have already made millions, but the truth is that after selling 30,000 games we are still in debt.

Events soon taught me that success in business could be won only if I acted in a business-like manner: excessively friendly when I needed something or someone and curt and exacting when it was the other way around. I developed painful physical symptoms, slept less, continued scheming into my dreams, started noticing when my workers (all close friends) arrived late for work, worried about corporate taxes and became a crashing bore at parties, where all I wanted to talk about was my game. Activities I normally enjoyed began to pale in comparison to the newly discovered thrill of making a big sale, and I found myself thinking of humanity more and more in terms of customers and potential customers.

Unlike the overnight metamorphosis of the salesman in Kafka's story into a cockroach, my own frighteningly similar change took place slowly, and I hope it is still not complete. At first, I was bemused by the strange feelings that began to disrupt my professorial calm, certain that I remained in control.

I should have known better, for Marx had already warned how functions get hold of people and drive them against their will to become something they are not. The process is one of "embodiment." The capitalist, for Marx, is not a real individual as much as the socioeconomic functions of owning means of production and exploiting workers and consumers in search of profits. These functions—summed up in "capital" (or wealth used with the sole aim of creating more wealth)— belong to the capitalist system and pre-date the individual capitalist, who comes to embody them. It is the pressure of these functions, of what is required to perform them effectively, that subtly and insidiously transforms the real individual into someone who only sees other people as a means to make money.

Caught in a whirlwind that is not of their own making, capitalists too—though most will not recognize it—are but victims of an inhuman system. If I have long known that socialism would be good for workers, I now understand just how much capitalists, as human beings, have to gain from a system that serves social needs instead of private profits. *Socialism humanizes.* I intend to carry this message of hope to the next meeting of my Chamber of Commerce.

> *Postscript* (two years later): The New York Chamber of Commerce did not react very favorably to my message of hope, but Warner Brothers did to the extent of purchasing my life story to do a film on the *Class Struggle* game. After preparing a disastrous anti-socialist script, the idea was dropped, and I learned another painful lesson about the world of business.

‡ In Oral Exams, if you have a choice, try to begin the questioning in your strongest field. This will build up your confidence, and also help impress teachers with your performance from the start. Early impressions tend to last and affect a teacher's reaction to whatever comes after. (I've just come back from an oral exam, where an excellent student ignored this advice, and chose to deal with her weakest subject area first. "Just to get it over with," she said. What a disaster!)

What's waiting for you after college? Let's assume you're lucky and you find a job. Let's further assume—a big assumption—that it is a full time and permanent job (a growing number of new jobs are only part-time or temporary). Let's really stick our neck out and assume that the wages are not too bad (most jobs pay less than they used to and most new jobs fall into the lowest wage category). Well, after so much good luck, where does that leave you? Welcome to "Job Stress," whose symptoms include: exhaustion, anger, anxiety, muscle pains, headaches, insomnia and digestive disorders. As far back as 1991, 72% of America's workers were found to be suffering from one or another version of this complaint. (*International Herald Tribune*, July 11, 1991) And all this only if you're "lucky."

Among the causes of stress as determined by this survey were "a substantial reduction in employee benefits...elimination of positions at the company...frequent requirements for overtime," and a lack of control over one's job. All of these conditions have worsened in the past decade, and in particular the number of hours that people with full time jobs are forced to work. A recent study showed that between 1983-1997 women in married couples increased their work load by 223 hours a year (that's nearly 6 weeks) and men in married couples by 158 hours (4 weeks), which makes Americans with full time jobs the most overworked workers in the developed countries. Another First for Uncle Sam. In short, our capitalists do whatever is required (and they can get away with) to maximize their profits, no matter its effect on workers' health and well being.

I'm sorry to have to be the one to tell you that your "higher education" probably won't get you the job you've been preparing for, because most good jobs have been automated, computerized, broken into part-time, flexible and temporary jobs, exported to countries where the pay is much less, and/or made into stressful horrors. But getting a "higher education" does give you a little time to think about whether this is the kind of world you want to live in and whether we as a people can do better. Are you making good use of this opportunity?

‡ So you failed the exam (or got a grade lower than you wanted, which many students experience as just as bad). It happens, and it isn't the end of the world, not even your world. What's a "How To" book on exams doing talking about failure? Well, aside from making this tiny effort to keep things in proportion, I want to stress the extraordinary learning opportunity occasional failure can provide. When else is all that we must do to improve set out so clearly? For the rest, it is worth recalling (and it may be the only true thing Nixon ever said): "It is when the going gets tough that the tough get going."

If you can't find a good job, many of you are thinking, you can always start a small business. Right? Doesn't the "American Dream" say that if you have a good idea, invest your whole kitty in it, and work like a demon, you too can get rich? All people have to do is try. And they do, or want to. A poll of workers on an assembly line in Detroit showed that over 80% of them had either been in business or were planning to start one. Horatio Alger lives on in people's imagination as a final and desperate hope, the only way of moving up in a society that insists we march through life in single file (collective solutions *verbotten*). Poor

Horatio. If he was really a typical small businessman, he probably went bust, strangled his cat or his kid, and finished his life in a factory (if he was lucky) or sponging on the Bowery. For bankruptcy, as all too many who take this route will learn, is also as American as apple pie—especially today with the money owed to banks and credit card companies going through the roof.

According to a Dun and Bradstreet survey of "experts," most business failures are due to the "lack of business-management knowledge." But this is like saying that the people on the Titanic drowned because they couldn't swim. The boat sank—remember? Likewise, with nine out of ten small businesses failing within ten years of getting started, the odds of succeeding are very small, even in the best of times. No doubt being a good manager contributes to the success of those few who make it, but so do a deep pocket, gross overwork and a willingness to lie and exploit others (including one's spouse and kids).

Ideologically, small business (even more than the existence of "free land" in the 19th century, and the relatively easy access to higher education today) puts flesh on the idea of equality of opportunity, the core rationalization on which democratic capitalism stands or falls. It is only because most people believe that they really have a chance to become rich and respected that they can view their present setbacks as temporary. No wonder most American workers cannot admit that they belong to the working class, that they have settled there for good.

Consequently, capitalism repeats the same lie in a thousand ways, lauds the "entrepreneurial spirit" without cessation, and pulls one unlikely small business success story after another out of its media hat to show not only that it can be done but that *you* can do it.

‡ On All Exams, if you can't answer the questions, don't assume that the fault is always (or only) yours. "I'm surprised I didn't get more wrong. Those questions were so confusing," said Raffaele Costa, Italy's Minister of Transport, when he flunked his country's new written driver's test, a test prepared by "experts" in his ministry.

If an exam question doesn't make any sense, don't hesitate to ask the teacher about it—immediately. Recognizing his/her error, the teacher may rephrase the question. This could happen even if the question is not all that confusing, in which case you'll have a lot more to go on in developing your answer.

"Globalization" is but another name for capitalism, but it's capitalism with the gloves off and on a world scale. It is capitalism at a time when all the old restrictions and inhibitions have been or are in the process of being put aside, a supremely self-confident capitalism, one without apparent rivals and therefore without a need to compromise or apologize.

The main features of capitalism in its stage of globalization include: 1) free trade; 2) free movement of capital; 3) the easy relocation of industries across national borders in pursuit of lower labor costs, lower taxes and fewer pollution controls; 4) the rise in influence of financial capital, and the banks and Treasury Ministries that represent it, over industrial and commercial capital, and the institutions that represent them; 5) a spectacular increase in personal debt as a springboard for heightened consumption; 6) growth in the number and size of business mergers both nationally and internationally, followed invariably by radical restructuring and downsizing of the labor force; 7) in the stock market, "financial instruments"—national currencies, insurance, debts, commodity futures, etc.—take over from the production of real goods as the main targets of investment, making the stock market more of a casino than ever; 8) the rapid flow of advertising, public relations, infotainment, and spin into all walks of life, including education; 9) the replacement of many full time jobs with temporary and part-time jobs, and the spread of outsourcing and contract labor; 10) a quantum increase in the speed at which information, particularly information relevant to profit making, moves around the globe;

11) minimal taxes on business; 12) deregulation of business practices that harm workers, consumers and communities; 13) attacks on the economic welfare and security reforms of the past century mainly to reduce business taxes but also to increase the number of workers willing to work for very low wages; 14) privatization of many formerly public institutions and functions (except, of course, the police and the army); 15) the spread of "accountability," quantitatively measurable and interpreted from a managerial point of view, to all sectors of society, including education; 16) the widening of social and economic inequality beyond anything seen in the capitalist era; 17) the weakening of all independent organs of the working class; 18) the weakening of the national state (and therefore of democratic control) in areas where capitalists never wanted the state to exercise much control in the first place; and 19) the creation and strengthening of various international institutions—like the I.M.F., the World Bank, the W.T.O., the Davos Conference (see Chapter l) and N.A.T.O.—to

coordinate, make propaganda for and enforce our still hesitant participation in all these developments. Oh, and 20) exams, lots of exams, everywhere—to prepare the next generation, of course, for all the new slots that have been created, but also to insure that they perform uncomplainingly once slotted.

Taken together, these developments—which are all internally related—constitute a new stage in capitalism. It is a serious error to think that they have brought us beyond capitalism. If anything, with these changes, our society is more thoroughly capitalist than ever before. After all, more and more of the world is privately owned, more and more wealth is devoted to maximizing profits rather than serving needs (and only serving needs in so far as they maximize profits), more and more people sell their labor power in order to live, more and more objects (ideational as well as material) carry price tags and can be

bought in the market, and money and those who have a lot of it have more power and status then ever before. This is capitalism, capitalism with a vengeance, and that's globalization. Which means, too, that the problems associated with globalization cannot be solved—as so many liberals would like to do—without dealing with their roots in the capitalist system.

So, has capitalism changed a lot since Marx's day? Yes, of course. Is Marx's analysis still relevant? Just because of these changes, it is more relevant now than ever.

‡ In Studying for an exam, how important is *sleep*? The *Journal of Cognitive Neural Science* (March, 2000) published a study that shows a clear link between an enhanced memory and a good night's sleep. The best results were achieved by students who slept eight hours. More sleep also enabled students to remember skills as well as facts longer than those who slept less. Harvard Professor Robert Stickgold, who directed the study, goes so far as to claim, "How well Harvard undergraduates do on the next day on a retest does not depend on what preparatory school they went to, their SAT scores, or how hard they tried. Rather, it mostly depends on how well they slept."

Of course, this assumes that the student has already encountered the material that will be on the exam, while a good deal of late-night cramming is to catch up on things that one hasn't had a chance to look at. Still, Stickgold's study makes it clear that getting a good night's sleep before an exam is an integral part of preparing for it, which means—among other things—that you should try to finish all new reading at least a day before the exam. As for Oral Exams, besides giving you the air of a zombie, cramming all night leads to a stumbling and dispirited performance. It is also bad for your health.

EIGHT

A principal in a Newark high school, Joe Clark, made a national reputation for himself by bringing peace and quiet to his school. His solution was to expel all the troublemakers. But this same action led to an increase in crime in the surrounding neighborhood, as the troublemakers simply plied their trade elsewhere. It's the musical chairs approach to social problems that is so favored by liberals.

Liberals are people who recognize most of our social problems and truly want to do something about them. They view these problems as existing separate from each other and believe they can be dealt with one at a time. If these problems are internally related, however, then trying to solve any one alone will prove impossible and may even, as we saw in the case of Joe Clark, make the other problems worse. Recognizing that our major social problems are interconnected and can only be solved together is the insight that turns liberals into radicals. (It happened to me) And solving these problems together means getting rid of the social system, capitalism, that gives rise to most of them. By explaining how this system came about and how it functions, Marxism fills out this radical insight and helps us develop a strategy for fundamental change.

> "A liberal sees a beggar on the street and says the system is not working. A Marxist sees a beggar on the street and says it is."
> —Bill Livant

‡ In Essay Exams, if you run out of time, give a brief outline of whatever you can't finish. This should be enough to show that you really do know the answer and what you might have done if you had more time. With such an outline, many teachers will feel justified in weighing your completed answers more heavily than they otherwise would in determining your overall grade.

Conservatives? In the U.S. at least, these are people who are so busy blaming the victims of our social problems for their suffering that they have difficulty recognizing that these problems even exist. They divide into those who are materially quite comfortable and don't want to be disturbed by the din caused by those who are not, those who are materially very insecure and fear the competition of those right behind them on the social ladder, and those who are simply full of hate and prejudice for whomever is different and whatever is new. Rather than wishing to preserve existing conditions, most American conservatives want to go back to an idealized version of the "good old days," when dissatisfied folks suffered in silence, that exists only in their imagination. Consequently, "reactionaries" would be a much more accurate name for them.

What about such conservative virtues as small government, fiscal restraint, individual responsibility and family values? Yes, conservatives talk about these things, but for most it's only a fig leaf, a series of homilies put together by the public relations firm that constructs their election platforms. Few so called "conservatives" oppose the expansion of government when it serves their interests, or turn down a handout when it is they who receive it. The biggest "welfare queens" in our society are the rich, most of them conservatives, who prefer to get their welfare checks in the form of state subsidies, tax write-offs, guaranteed prices, etc. Our colossal national debt was the product of Reagan's conservative Government. And family values? Well, conservative families, as we can read even in the capitalist press, are in no better shape than anyone else's. Hence, the essence of conservatism is not to be found in what they say, but in what they do and why they do it. And what they do is defend their power and material privileges however they can—including mis-presenting what they want—out of a combination of selfishness, insecurity and prejudice.

‡ In All Kinds of Exams, whenever you are given both a text and a question and told to read the text first, it is generally wise to disregard this instruction and to read the question first, at least quickly. This will enable you to avoid getting bogged down with complexities in the text that have little or nothing to do with the question. Of course, when you finish reading the text, you must re-read the question, and more slowly this time.

"All they think about is money..."

What are the capitalists really like? Marx and Luther, who agree on practically nothing else, see eye to eye on this. According to Marx, "No eunuch flatters his despot more basely or uses more despicable means to stimulate his dulled capacity for pleasure in order to sneak a favor for himself than does the industrial eunuch—the producer—in order to sneak for himself a few pennies, in order to charm the golden bird out of the pockets of his Christianity-beloved neighbors. He puts himself at the service of the other's most depraved fancies, plays the pimp between him and his needs, excites in him morbid appetites, lies in wait for each of his weaknesses—all so he can demand cash for his services of love."

While Luther says that businessmen "have learned the trick of placing such commodities as pepper, ginger and saffron in damp vaults or cellars in order to increase the weight...Nor is there a single article of trade whatever out of which they cannot make unfair profit by false measuring, counting or weighing. They produce artificial colors, or they put pretty things at the top and bottom and the ugly ones in the middle, and indeed there is no end to their trickery, and no one tradesman will trust another, for they know each other's ways."

But is it the capitalists who make the capitalist system what it is, or the system that makes the capitalists act as they do? The economist, Howard Sherman, has constructed a fable to help us answer this crucial question.

> "Suppose a landlord decided to be kind to a poor tenant and collect no rent. The Landlord would be unable to pay the mortgage and the bank would take over. Suppose the director of the bank that owned the mortgage decided to be kind to the kind landlord and not replace him. In that case, profits would fall, and the bank director would be replaced. Suppose by the furthest stretch of the imagination that the stockholders in the banking firm decided to be kind and not fire the bank director. Then the bank would eventually go bankrupt, and a new bank would take over the mortgage and fire all the kind people."

The problem, it would appear, is not that the people in power are greedy and heartless, though some obviously are, but that the rules by which they play—and by which we are all forced to play—reward venality and penalize kindness. With the imperative to maximize profits front and center, it is these rules of the game (themselves rooted in the very nature of capital as self-expanding value or wealth) that need to be changed. But let's not be fooled. We won't be able to change these rules until the people who benefit from them, the capitalist class, are themselves removed from power.

‡ Memorizing Important Facts for an exam. There are no sure fire techniques, but some combination of the following helps: 1) writing the facts down a few times, in summary form if need be and preferably in your own words; 2) reading them out loud to someone else or even to yourself; 3) trying to state the facts without looking at them, and repeating the exercise until you are successful; 4) relating the facts to the context, or problem, or debate in which they appear (perhaps the most important step of all); 5) if the facts are complicated, fixing the connections in mind by associating them with parts of a structure (like a house) or a system (like the human body) with which you are familiar; and 6) looking for one or more code words either in the facts or in something they suggest to you, possibly even a number, that are easier to remember, and which can be used to recall the facts when you need them.

It is also worth noting that facts reviewed a few times over the course of the term are easier to remember than facts learned during last minute cramming. And if you're under the illusion that you remember things better with the help of loud music, or a couple of drinks, or a little weed, or a sleepless night, forget it. All this being said, it is my impression that in courses that require a lot of thinking, students devote too much time when preparing for exams to memorizing the bare facts and too little time to interpreting them and to using them for resolving problems that are likely to come up.

For your other courses, which—unfortunately—probably means most of the courses you're taking, don't neglect to memorize all the basic facts and especially those whose importance has been underlined by your teacher.

Since 1947, the world has spent over $15 trillion on arms, that's 15 thousand billion. About 1/2 has been spent by the U.S., 1/4 by the U.S.S.R. and Russia, and 1/4 by the rest of the world. To get some idea of the magnitude of this sum, it has been estimated that 1/2 of it (or just the amount spent by the U.S.) would be enough to industrialize the entire third world up to the level of France, with a minimum of pollution. Who says the world isn't rich enough to eliminate poverty, illiteracy, and most forms of disease? It's just that our leaders over the last half century have been more interested in producing weapons of mass destruction and maximizing the profits of weapons' manufacturers. Imagine all the good we could do with this wealth if we put other leaders with other priorities in their place.

‡ In Essay Exams, take a little time at the start (ten minutes in an hour exam is not too much) to outline your answers. If possible, this should include your beginning, your conclusion, and the main points and/or arguments that you hope will take you from the one to the other, maybe simply listing some of the authors to be brought in along the way. Students differ as to how detailed an outline they need or are capable of before they actually start writing. As someone—I can't recall who—once remarked, writing is "a raid on the inarticulate." We often discover how to say something only in the process of saying it. So don't worry too much if you can't produce a full outline before starting out on your answer, and don't feel overly restricted by your outline if while writing your thoughts carry you in another direction.

Who said the following: "In as much as most good things are produced by labor, it follows that all such things of right belong to those whose labor has produced them. But it has so happened in all ages of the world that some have labored and others have without labor enjoyed a large proportion of the fruits. This is wrong and should not continue. To secure each laborer the whole product of his labor, or as nearly as possible, is a worthy object of any good Government."

If your answer is Karl Marx, just because it sounds a lot like his labor theory of value, well—you're wrong. Not that it doesn't sound like Marx's theory, because it does. But the person who said it is Abraham Lincoln (from a 1847 speech). You may also be surprised to learn that this same president said, "These capitalists generally act, harmoniously and in concert, to fleece the people." (1837)

‡ Take-Home Exams: Teachers will sometimes hand out an exam, usually an Essay Exam, and give you a week or more in which to complete it. Write the outlines and if possible the first drafts of your answers as soon as you receive the questions, so you can use most of the time to reflect on what you've written. For some subjects, our best thinking occurs over a period of days, whether in the development of or in reaction to our first thoughts. This has certainly been my experience in writing anything, including this book.

Take-Home Exams are, generally, more difficult than other exams, because it is impossible to limit the amount of time that some students will spend on them. That means longer and more detailed answers from at least some of the competition. There is always a grading curve of some sort no matter what your teacher says or even tries to do. Teachers can't help but be affected by the general level of most of the class and, to a lesser degree, by the very best and very worst exams they grade. So if you know beforehand that many of your peers are going to perform better than usual, as invariably occurs with take home exams, then it is important that you do better as well. Whatever the amount of time your teacher suggests that you spend on a take home exam, therefore, it is wise to up it by a third.

Who said the following: "For whatever we say of other motives, we must never forget that in the main the ordinary conduct of man is determined by economic motives...Business is the foundation of every other relation, particularly the political relation." If your answer is Karl Marx, just because it sounds a lot like what is popularly (never by Marx) called economic determinism, well—you're wrong. Not that it doesn't sound like Marx's views, because it does. But the person who said it is Woodrow Wilson. You may also be surprised to learn that this same president also said, "The truth is we are all caught up in a great economic system which is heartless."

‡ Exam Grades: Does it ever pay to complain about a grade? Sure, depending, of course, on the teacher and the reason for complaint (or the excuse you have for not doing as well as you could have). If for any reason you believe your grade is less that what it should be, you should not hesitate to tell the teacher. But try to do so in as non-confrontational a way as possible. No teacher wants to give in to what appears like a demand or to respond positively to what sounds like an insult.

Teachers don't like to admit that they are open to changing a grade, because they are afraid of receiving a flood of complaints. Still, don't take their public proclamation on this subject as their last word. There are always exceptions, and you may be one. I've changed many grades after hearing students' complaints, and never—I should add—in a downward direction.

Who said the following: "In the councils of Government, we must guard against the acquisition of unwarranted influence, whether sought or unsought, by the military-industrial complex. The potential for the disastrous rise of misplaced power exists and will persist." This one doesn't sound like Marx, but it does sound like some kind of radical, doesn't it? Well, it was Dwight Eisenhower. (Farewell Address, 1961)

What's going on here? How can all these presidents (and there are other presidents I could have cited) hold such radical, even Marxist views? The answer is that virtually everyone, no matter how conservative, has some radical ideas and insights, that is ideas which go to the roots of a problem and indicate how our society really works. The evidence for the roots of some problems is just so overwhelming. But—and this is the catch—these ideas remain isolated. They don't connect up with other radical ideas into a pattern, into a larger picture. Instead, they just hang there, surrounded by more superficial thoughts, and consequently never have a serious effect on one's overall understanding and behavior. None of these presidents, for example, ever took any radical actions based on their isolated radical insights. Obviously, what's needed is to connect up a number of these insights until they make up a pattern, until we see how each leads to the others, and is in fact part of the others. That pattern would then represent the structure of our society, understood as what sets limits for and gives a deeper sense and direction to most of the seemingly disconnected events that make up our daily lives.

Marx's main contribution was to reveal this pattern. That's why he occupies a privileged place in our study, and why I have devoted more attention throughout to uncovering connections than to laying out the bare facts. And that's also why defenders of the status quo work so hard at blurring, masking and denying these same connections (and rejecting Marx), in the fear that once people who are dissatisfied with the *status quo* grasp the pattern they will not only set out to change it but will know what to do.

‡ You really should be wearing combat fatigues and probably a helmet, because—as you will have figured out by now—school is a battleground, and it has nothing to do with knives and guns. And you, poor, unsuspecting students, are—willy, nilly—not only participants but also the ground on which most battles are fought as well as the major prize for which the opposing sides are contending. Everything that happens to you in school conspires to pull you this way or that. No one and nothing is neutral, and for the moment—and it's been a long one—those who would mold you into docile workers for your future employers occupy all the heights. They

use their power to fill your schedules with narrow, required courses full of the information and skills that *they* need, hire mostly safe professors to teach them, reward conformity and punish dissent, and keep you busy preparing for one T.V. quiz show after another, which they call exams.

Yet, the university remains contested terrain. For to convince you that all this adds up to an education, our rulers have to allow some radical voices to be heard. This gives the appearance that there is open debate. Otherwise, you might mistake your university for just another Bible college, and develop an unhealthy skepticism toward all that you're learning, most of which our leaders not only want you to know but to believe in. To be fair, there are some on the other side who truly value academic freedom and even enjoy the intellectual challenge that radicals pose. Still, on the whole, radicals are tolerated in academia in order to legitimate the bulk of what gets taught there, which is to say, to fool you better.

We radicals, on the other hand, try to use the little space and time allotted us to raise embarrassing questions and, where possible, offer unorthodox answers. It is an unfair fight, since those who run our universities have all the big weapons, but how long can students ignore the fact that the shoes into which they will step after graduation are already so tight that most of the people wearing them can hardly walk? And, life in capitalism being what it is, the fit is getting tighter and tighter. Anybody for a change of shoes?

NINE

‡ Someone once defined an exam answer as something that passes from the mouth of the lecturer to the hand of the student without ever passing through the student's brain. A blood libel? I wish I could be so sure. Listen to this story.

Everyone knows that people are gullible, but few would include themselves in this generalization. With the aim of showing students that they accept more on authority than they realize, I often open my undergraduate course on the history of political theory with a nonsense lecture. I tell students that I want to test how well they can understand a new and difficult subject by spending the first twenty minutes on an exciting new departure called "Proportional Political Theory." Afterwards, I tell the class to write for fifteen minutes on the question, "What is Proportional Political Theory and what do you think of it?"

Without going into particulars, suffice it to say that "P.P.T." is based on the principle that "Politics is the logic of the political mind," from which it follows that each thinker can be represented by a combination of numbers and letters. I then proceed to add Locke and Rousseau to get Marx, and to subtract Aristotle from Plato to get—who else?—Mill, and so on.

When the papers are collected, I ask students if any of them wrote that I was speaking nonsense. A few hands are raised, but from the rest, nothing. Most students, perhaps 90%, are quite shocked by my revelation. There is some nervous laughter, and a few people get angry. My response is to point out how important it is to think critically about what we hear (or read), because—well, look at what can happen when you don't. And who is to say that this is the first time they have accepted as true some utter nonsense just because it came from an "authority"? Could it be, I ask, that this has also happened with other teachers, with newscasters and reporters, politicians, priest/ministers/rabbis, and even parents? At least in this case I have confessed to speaking nonsense, but what of the others? And how can they, the students, know? I would be very frightened, I add, if I were them, because their heads may be bulging with nonsense told to them by others whom they respected a little too much.

The lively discussion that follows is devoted equally to hearing alibis and to looking at what in students' socialization has so dampened their critical spirits. I then promise that I will never knowingly speak nonsense to them again, but it is only they—by insisting that everything that is told to them make sense—who will be able to judge whether I keep my promise. Later on, in correcting the work they do for the course, I am very attentive to the slightest sign that a student is thinking for him/herself even to the point of giving higher grades to those who disagree with my arguments—assuming that they know them—than to those who simply repeat what I said.

What lessons can be drawn from this story for taking exams or writing papers for *your* teachers? It all depends, I guess, on how much they want you to think, really think, for yourself. Well, what have your teachers said or done recently that indicates the importance they attach to critical thinking? If nothing, watch out.

Until the middle of the 19th century one of the biggest killers of women was puerperal fever contracted in childbirth. The cause of the infection was the doctors, who never washed their hands before delivering a baby. Dr. Philip Semelweiss, a Hungarian doctor, was the first to make the connection between these two events. When, on his instigation, the interns in the hospital where he worked did wash their hands, the cases of puerperal fever practically disappeared. The evidence he gathered seemed conclusive. Unfortunately, it was several decades before Louis Pasteur developed his theory of germs, which meant that while Semelweiss was clearly right he couldn't explain why he was right. There was no theory available that made sense of what he found. The result was that virtually the entire medical establishment refused to take Semelweiss' life saving discovery seriously, despite all the evidence —including statistical evidence—that he had gathered. They refused to believe what they were hearing, because they had no theoretical framework in which to put it. Such is the importance of theory.

Many people in our society have noted the connection between the growing wealth of the few and the increasing misery of the many, between the interests of the capitalist class and the actions of the Government, between having money and being free, between being poor and being powerless. As we saw, these insights are not limited to Marx and Marxists: even American presidents have had them. Despite this, most people don't take these observations very seriously. Lacking a theory to make sense of what they are seeing—they don't know what importance to give it—growing numbers stop seeing it, or forget what they've just seen, or ennoble their confusion by calling it a "paradox." Marxism supplies the needed theory, but what kind of theory is it?

‡ In Essay Exams, students are often given a choice of questions to answer, as in "Answer 4 out of 7 of the following..." It is not necessary to choose all your questions at the start. It's very common to have doubts, for example, as to which should be your last one of two questions. Don't let that worry you. You may even need to answer one or two questions for your thinking on the others to proceed far enough to make the best choices.

In *The Man Who Mistook His Wife for a Hat*, Dr. Oliver Sacks tells of a brain injured patient of his who lost his ability to perceive patterns. He could see aspects of things well enough, but he couldn't put them together. Because most things only make sense as parts of something larger than themselves, he couldn't tell what anything was. He couldn't recognize faces, for example.

The malady that Sacks uncovered is far more widespread than he feared, except for most people the cause is neither biological or psychological but rather sociological and historical. In sum, the socialization that we all undergo in capitalism inclines us to see the particulars that enter our lives but to ignore the ways they are related and, thus, to miss the patterns that emerge from these relations. The social sciences reinforce this tendency, first, by breaking up the totality of human knowledge into the specialized learning of competing disciplines, each with its own distinctive language, and, second, as part of their stress on quantitative techniques, by concentrating almost exclusively on the bits and pieces of our experience that permit statistical manipulation.

This book is full of "patterns" that most people in our society are socialized not to see. Such is the connections between the working class and the capitalist class, between the interests of the capitalists and how our government works, between feelings of alienation and the power of money (upcoming), and there are many others. In every case, most people see the parts well enough but not the connections and not the overall pattern, or capitalism, which is made up of the sum of these connections. Capitalism, as such, is virtually invisible in the social sciences. Yet, it is only the connections and the resulting pattern—as in the case of Dr. Sack's patient—that gives meaning and value to the parts. In an instant, all sorts of "paradoxes" and mysteries—like growing poverty in the midst of growing wealth—make sense. ("This is what capitalism is. This is how it looks. This is how it works.") But it is a sense that those who run our society and determine our socialization (including your education) would prefer we didn't get.

As regards the form, this separation—repeated on a hundred fronts—of what cannot be separated without distortion is the key feature of what is called "un-dialectical" thought. "Dialectical" thinking, on the other hand, is the ongoing effort to grasp things in terms of their interconnections and this includes their ties with their own preconditions and future possibilities as well as with whatever is affecting them (and whatever they are affecting) right now. The whole panoply of otherwise confusing dialectical concepts—such as "contradiction," "totality," "abstraction," etc., (which I have tried to spare readers of this book)—is directed to making some group of interconnections easier to think about. To make more and better sense out of the trivia, paradoxes, half-truths and outright nonsense that constitutes such a large part of most people's understanding of society, therefore, requires not only a lot of facts that are generally hidden from us but a more dialectical grasp of the facts we already know.

‡

RULES FOR WRITING

by Steve Rubin

1) Each pronoun has to agree with their antecedent.
2) Just between you and I, case is important.
3) Verbs has to agree with their subjects.
4) Watch out for irregular verbs that have cropped into our language.
5) Do not use no double negatives.
6) When dangling, do not use participles.
7) Join clauses good, like a conjunction should.
8) Be careful of run-on sentences they have to be punctuated.
9) About sentence fragments
10) In letters themes reports articles and other writings commas are used to keep a string of items apart.
11) Do not use commas, that are not necessary.

12) Its important to use apostrophe's correctly.
13) Do not abbrev. unless the meaning is clear.
14) Check to see if you any words out.
15) An author when he is writing should not get into the habit of making use of too many unnecessary words that really are not needed.
16) Never use a preposition to end a sentence with.
17) Always spell out numbers from 1 to 10.
18) The active voice is preferred by most writers.
19) But of course, a conjunction cannot be used at the beginning of a sentence.
20) Last but not least, lay off clichés.

Okay, be honest now. At what number did you notice that each rule embodies the very mistake it identifies? If you got past five, you're in trouble. If you made it to ten, you need help with reading, English grammar, or both. If you made it all the way to twenty, maybe you should consider writing in another language. Alternatively, you may just have a bad authority hangup with teachers, so that you can't imagine that they would commit such errors. This is akin to the gullibility so many students showed in believing my nonsense lecture (above). In either case, now that you know the extent of your problem, you can get busy working on it. Incidentally, there are exceptions to most of these "good writing" rules (as you will have noticed from reading this book), but you have to know the rule to sense when you can get away with an exception.

Do you suffer from the feeling of being disconnected from the world around you, of isolation, of not belonging, of no one caring, of being an outsider, and therefore of being ineffectual and powerless? If so, you've got lots of company. This is one of the greatest mysteries of our time, since it is not clear where this "normal suffering" comes from. Another equally big mystery has to do with the extraordinary power of money in our society and the willingness of most people to do virtually anything to acquire it.

These two mysteries don't seem to have much in common, but Marx treats both of them as aspects of the problem he calls "alienation." Many psychologists and sociologists use this term, but they limit the meaning of "alienation" to some version of the psychological malaise given above. What is crucial for Marx, on the other hand, is the overall situation of the person who has these feelings, and, in particular, the part played by money. In his discussion of alienation, this is brought out by focusing on four relations that lie at the heart of the work experience in our society: 1) the relation between the individual and his/her productive activity, in which others determine how it is done, under what conditions, at what speed, and for what wage or salary, and even if and when it is to begin and end; 2) the relation between the individual and the product of that activity, in which others control and use the product for their own purposes (making something does not confer any right to use what one has made); 3) the relation between the individual and other people, particularly with those who control both one's productive activity and its products, where each side pursues their own interests without considering the effect of their actions on the other (mutual indifference and competition becomes the characteristic forms of human interaction); and 4) the relation between the individual and the species, or with what it means to be a human being. For Marx, the ties between an individual and his productive activities, products, and the other people with whom he cooperates at work are essential aspects of human nature. To cut these ties, which is what happens when any element in this cluster is removed from one's control, is to deprive people of a good deal of their potential for coordinated growth and development and to leave them humanly diminished.

Though Marx's discussion of alienation is centered on the sphere of production, these four relations can also be found in other areas of capitalist life—in education, politics, culture, science and religion—

wherever, in fact, people's activities and products (including services and ideas) are under the control of others who use them to further their own special interests. In this way, for example, students whose distinctive activities include coming to lectures, taking exams, paying tuition, etc. can be seen as producing a range of "products" that include grades, diplomas, professors and the university itself. Through activities of relating to "this" building as a university, it is they (you) who turn it into one. Otherwise, it is simply an ordinary building. The same with the talkative man or woman who is turned into a professor by your treating him/her as such.

Both of these activities and products are under the control of the higher administrations and boards of trustees of our universities, who cleverly manipulate them in the service of their own interests with relative indifference to the real interests of the students. The result is that students are cut off from and have little to say over the entire university context that constitutes so much of their lives as students. Yet, this context is an essential part of who they are as human beings (aspects of what Marx considers their broader human nature) as well as of what they are as students. Diminished as people in the very act of manifesting their identity as students within the capitalist university, is it any wonder that most students feel disconnected, isolated and powerless?

What about the mysterious power of money? It is obvious that money can only buy what people are able and willing to sell. In our society, that includes virtually everything, but it does so only because most of the ties that have bound us to the world—to the products we make, to the activities that make them and the qualities of strength, judgement, intelligence used in making them, to the other people involved with us in the process—have been severed in alienated activity of one sort or another. People don't sell their limbs or other parts of themselves that are considered essential to who and what they are. So in feudalism, for example, serfs—who suffer another form of domination—could not sell their labor power or the products of their labor. They wouldn't even think of doing so. But as people got separated from their own qualities, conditions, activities and products by the alienation described above, the portion of the world and of our life in the world that became available for sale grew and with it the power of money to buy it.

Money, in other words, only buys what people as a result of their alienation no longer are. Hence, Marx's striking reference to money as "the alienated ability of mankind." It is the ability and qualities we had and lost that now confront us in the mysterious form of money. It's power is our own power that has been taken from us, mystified, reified and turned against us in the hands of those, the rich, who have interests that are opposed to our own. When a *New Yorker* cartoon says, "Money is life's report card," it informs us not only on how much better some are doing than others in capitalism but on how poorly we are all doing in life.

The history of capitalism can be told as a story of how human beings through their alienation have become progressively less human, less connected to and with less control over all that distinguish us as a species from the rest of the animal world (hence, increasingly isolated and powerless), and how more and more of what we need to live has become the private property of others ("Things are in the saddle and they ride mankind" in the words of the poet Wordsworth). Or, this same history can be recounted as a story of how money has acquired ever greater power over people as the only means by which we can get others, who are in a similar fix, to provide us with the necessities of life that we no longer control. The two mysteries with which we began—people's feelings of isolation and powerlessness and the extraordinary power of money—are easily resolved once we recognize they make up two sides of the same phenomenon, which is but the alienated life process of capitalist society.

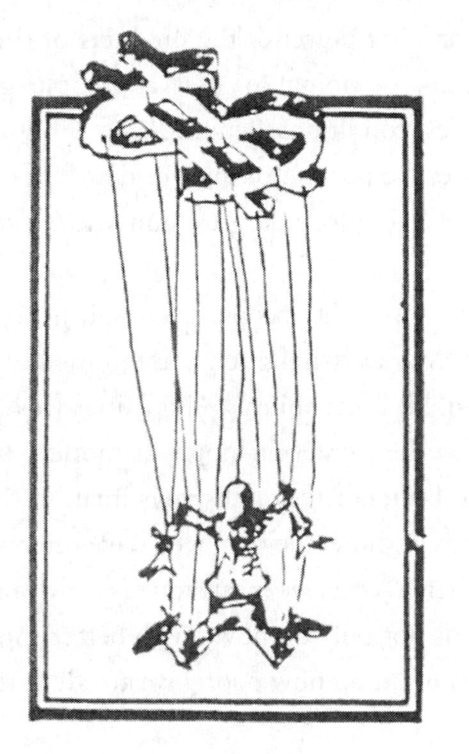

‡ Studying. What kind of exam does your teacher give? Don't rely only on what he/she says. Ask students who have taken the course before; examine the course evaluations that may have been put out by the professor's department or by the Student Government; and try to get hold of exams from previous years. The fewer surprises you have on seeing the exam, the better you are likely to do.

What is the relation between grades and money? In ancient Greek mythology, Procrustes was an inn keeper who made sure that guests fit perfectly into the bed he prepared for them. Those who were too short were stretched, while guests who were too tall had their legs trimmed to the size of the bed. Both money and grades serve our society as Procrustean beds. Money enables us to compare very different things on the basis of their price. Grades enable us to compare very different people on the basis of a letter. Once we attach a monetary value to something, its other qualities become much less important and are often ignored altogether. The same thing happens to the distinctive qualities of each person once we view him or her as an "A," "B," or "C" student.

"Commodification," is the process by which things acquire a price. What is made to be eaten, worn, lived in, etc. finds its way into the market and is hereafter thought about and valued largely in function of its price. Grades represent the commodification of the learning process. They stand in for many different kinds and levels of knowledge much like money does for the different kind of products it can buy. Grades reduce the enormous variety of human talent and achievement to a single dimension (what gets tested), then measures it, and eventually replaces it in the eyes of students, teachers and the general public alike. No wonder the grade consciousness of many students often reaches demented proportions, very much like the greed for money.

Grades could only acquire this power, because—as in the case of money—the activities they represent have become separated from and turned against the very people who are engaged in them. As we saw in the discussion of alienation above, everything students do as part of getting educated is controlled by those who run the universities and used primarily for their own benefit. Thus, exams break down students, viewed as a group of people who share a common interest in acquiring an education, into so many atomistic individuals competing for a limited good; while grading recombines the now isolated individuals into new, artificial groups ("A" students, "B" students, etc.), whose most distinctive qualities are of greatest interest to their future employers. More than a simple instrument of control, grades are the sign that academic servitude has arrived full circle. It is the form in which the relation of domination itself has passed into the hands of its victims, who are encouraged to treat the yellow star sown onto their jackets as if it were an Olympic gold medal.

IF YOU'RE NOT
OUTRAGED
YOU'RE NOT PAYING
ATTENTION
Johnny
Sincerely Yours,
Karl Marx
"Rebel with a cause."

TEN

A scientist who studies frogs wrote in his journal as follows:

> "Day one: I made a loud noise behind the frog, and he jumped 15 feet. Day two: I immobilized one of the frog's hind legs, and repeated the sound I made yesterday. The frog jumped only 3 feet. Day three: I immobilized both of the frog's hind legs, and made the same sound. The frog did not jump at all. Conclusion: When both of the frog's hind legs are immobilized, it goes deaf."

Social science has come up with many techniques to help our rulers sleep easier in their beds at night, but probably none is more worthy of the governmental and business support it receives than the widespread substitution of subjective reactions for the objective conditions that cause them. With this, capitalism is left off the hook. Much greater attention is also devoted to trivial problems, or the already obvious aspects of important ones, instead of to the things that we as hurting citizens need to know. Thus, a major study, reported in the *New York Times* (December 8, 1988), found that women do more housework than men, and another found a strong correlation between poverty and malnutrition. But there is still no large scale study of the relation between capitalism and the millions of unnecessary deaths and injuries that occur every year—unless we count the deceptive study done by the American Council of Life Insurance a few years back, which reported that people who lived longer than average tended to be "conservative, middle of the road." (Translation: "those with money.")

"Poverty is World's Greatest Killer," so ran a headline on the front page of the *Guardian Weekly* (May 7, 1995), one of England's leading liberal newspapers. A few weeks earlier, the same paper had a headline that said, "Rich Are Getting Richer, Poor Are Getting Poorer." The inescapable conclusion is that by taking an ever greater share of society's wealth, the rich are not just making the poor suffer more, they are actually killing them. The crime is murder, but on such a huge scale that most people have difficulty seeing it.

At a philosophy conference several years back, an errant hand wrote on a blackboard, "While radical philosophy points its finger at reality, mainstream philosophy studies the finger." And with certain honorable exceptions, so do political science, economics, psychology, sociology and even history.

‡ Cheating on Exams. Woody Allen confessed that he once got caught cheating on a metaphysics exam: "The professor saw me looking into the soul of the guy sitting next to me." Usually, it's more serious. A recent study by Professor Donald McCabe of Rutgers University shows that 41% of college students have cheated at least once on exams. This figure jumps to 76% for those planning careers in business. Also, students coming from families that make over $150,000 a year were found to cheat 50% more than students who came from families making under $25,000 a year. Where do you think the frequent cheaters picked up this behavior?

Congressman Jim Leach of Iowa tells the story of a star basketball player at Iowa State who went into the Burger King on campus with a rifle and no mask, and asked the kid who was serving for the cash. Just behind the counter was a photo of the basketball team in which this particular player was featured. When the clerk said, "Hi, big Sam," the robber responded, "It's not me."

WHAT DID YOU TELL THAT MAN JUST NOW
I TOLD HIM TO WORK FASTER!
HOW MUCH DO YOU PAY HIM?
FIFTEEN DOLLARS A DAY!
WHERE DO YOU GET THE MONEY TO PAY HIM?
I SELL PRODUCTS!
WHO MAKES THE PRODUCTS?
HE DOES!
HOW MANY PRODUCTS DOES HE MAKE IN ONE DAY?
FIFTY DOLLARS WORTH...
THEN INSTEAD OF YOU PAYING HIM HE PAYS YOU THIRTY FIVE DOLLARS A DAY TO TELL HIM TO WORK FASTER!
HUH?
WELL... I OWN THE MACHINES!
HOW DID YOU GET THE MACHINES?
I SOLD PRODUCTS AND BOUGHT THEM!
AND WHO MADE THOSE PRODUCTS?
SHUT UP... HE MIGHT HEAR YOU!

Well, there are some robberies where it's virtually impossible for the culprit to hide his identity, no matter how hard he tries. And there are others where a little sleuthing is required to learn who did it. Exploitation belongs to this second category. It is the capitalists taking from the workers a big chunk, often the biggest chunk, of the wealth the workers produce (everything, in fact, that is not returned to them in the form of wages or salaries). Exploring this theft, its preconditions and effects lies at the heart of Marx's political economy. When you think of all the people who are exploited, this is probably the biggest robbery in the entire history of the world.

The reason it is not immediately apparent who the thief is in the case of exploitation is that the bosses insist they have a right to a share of this new wealth. Don't they own the machines and raw materials used in production? It is their "private property." However, it doesn't take much sleuthing to uncover that this private property is simply the part of the wealth produced by earlier generations of workers that was never returned to them. In other words, what the capitalists got away stealing from our fathers and grandfathers provides them with the material basis (and—since they make the laws—the legal right) to continue helping themselves to the biggest part of what we produce today. Hence, the French anarchist Proudhon's famous cry, "Property is theft."

‡ In Essay and Oral Exams, there is an important difference between clarity and precision. While the nature of many answers, as Aristotle informs us, does not permit precision, there are few if any things about which we cannot be clear, including why it is often impossible to be precise. Teachers generally put a high value on clarity. In preparing for the exam, it is often useful to present answers to some of the questions you are expecting to a friend to see how well he understands you. Trying to teach what you know to others is, in any case, the ideal way of bringing the process of learning to a close (far better than taking an exam).

An airplane pilot announces to his passengers that he has two pieces of news to tell them. The good news is that they are traveling at the preestablished speed of 500 mph and all mechanisms on the plane are functioning perfectly. The bad news is that they are lost. Most radical critics of capitalism often sound like this. Capitalism, they say, produces a lot of goods very efficiently, but what kind of goods are they and who gets most of them? From all the suffering that one sees, it would appear that the system has lost its way.

Marx, on the other hand, would deny that the plane is lost. The capitalist system does quite nicely what its rulers intend it to do, which is to expand the forces of production while making the rich still richer. But the plane has serious and worsening engine problems, so that it is likely that it will soon fall from the sky. Capitalism is becoming impossible. Has it already?

‡ In Studying for an exam, it is essential to take an occasional break. For this, you have to know in a general way how much material there is to cover and, more precisely, how long you have to cover it. Breaks involve doing something else, anything else, that relieves the physical and psychological tension, and doesn't necessarily mean resting. The goal is to enable you to go back to studying with more energy and a greater ability to concentrate than you had when you stopped work. Don't begrudge yourself the breaks that you need. As much as possible, it is good to schedule your breaks beforehand.

Have you ever seen a chicken with its head cut off, how it runs wildly about, sometimes for several seconds, before it collapses and dies? If you are small and unlucky enough to be in its way, you can get badly hurt by these final gyrations. Capitalism is a lot like this chicken. It has died, but doesn't know it, and is flailing away in its death throes, causing terrible harm to everyone within striking distance.

Capitalism died the moment the conditions necessary for accumulating capital on the scale required by the enormous amount of wealth available for investment could no longer be assured. It died when the related conditions that are indispensable for selling all of the rapidly growing amount of finished goods likewise evolved out of reach. Today, there are simply not enough profitable investments in the production and distribution of goods, given the gigantic sums seeking such investments; nor are there enough people with sufficient purchasing power to buy the mountain of goods that have already been produced.

These problems also affect each other in the following way: Marx recognizes that all the wealth, or value, of society is produced by the workers, but they get back only part of it in their wages and salaries. The remainder, which Marx calls "surplus-value," is retained by the capitalists and is the source of all their wealth and power. With what they receive, the workers, who make up most of the consumers in society, buy back what they need to live, or rather that part of what they need that they can afford. This is always far less that what these same people, as workers, have produced. Now, while it is in the capitalists' interests that consumers have enough money to buy ever greater amounts of what the capitalists have to sell, it is also in the capitalists' interests to pay their workers as little wages as they can get away with, since this is how they maximize surplus-value. These two aims are in contradiction: the more surplus-value the capitalists succeed in extracting from their workers, the more difficulty they create for themselves when it comes to selling the finished commodities to these same people in their role as consumers. Think of it as a giant Catch 22 at the very core of the capitalist system.

Earlier, this worsening contradiction would lead to economic crisis and depression, and an eventual turn-around after enough of the accumulated wealth had been wasted or destroyed, often with the help of a major war. This would open up opportunities for new investment and for some new products, while increasing the profitability of those capitalist firms that were still in a position to provide them. However, in the present crisis, it appears that these in-house correctives are no longer available. In the age of nuclear weapons, a major war is unthinkable (and if it occurs, there will be no one around to reap the benefits), and minor wars, as have occurred in Viet Nam and the Gulf, do not destroy enough to play the same economic role in capitalism that was played by World Wars I and II. The alternatives that have arisen—like investment in the formerly "socialist" lands, the expansion of credit, space exploration, etc.—are simply too little to take up the enormous slack.

As for the generalized waste and destruction that goes on in any depression, the explosion in workers' productivity—aided by automation, computerization and robotization—is now so great that it is highly unlikely that capitalism will ever again need more workers than it currently employs, even when the need to replace what has been used up is added to present demands. On the contrary, unemployment, temporary employment and part-time employment are certain to grow world-wide, and probably very rapidly. All of which means that the workers as a class will be able to buy back proportionately fewer of their products in the future than they do now, driving capitalists to intensify still more the exploitation of workers with jobs (increasing the surplus-value extracted from them), while reducing even further the opportunities for profitable investment.

Deprived of the conditions necessary for its existence—in investment as in selling the finished product—the capitalist system can only go down hill, with its social and economic problems constantly worsening and becoming more intractable. Hence, the comparison of capitalism to a chicken that has already died but continues to flail around and cause injuries until, weakened beyond all recognition, it is finally put out of its misery.

The Indian historian, Ranagit Guha, once told me of an old Bengali proverb that says: If a cow gives a lot of milk, it's worth taking a few kicks. But if all it gives us is manure...Well, we are rapidly approaching this situation with capitalism, and the only question now is: how long will we accept the kicks?

‡ In Essay Exams, how important is the length of your answer? I recall a high school history teacher actually counting the number of pages I wrote for a term paper right in front of me, without reading any of it, before putting down the grade. Few teachers are this brazen, but as a rule longer answers do better, and not always because they contain more. However, when it becomes obvious that you are just taking up space and the teacher's valuable time, this could blow up in your face.

It's funny (sic) (sick?) how the Government has little trouble finding hundreds of billions of dollars to bail out such corporations as Chrysler, Continental Bank and the Savings and Loan Industry but can't find a fraction of this amount to improve our deteriorating schools, or to guarantee decent health care for everyone who needs it, or...Could it have something to do with the fact that most Cabinet members, Congressmen and Supreme Court Judges are personally wealthy and that businessmen and their hangers-on provide most of the money with which elections are fought? Too crude? Listen to what Senator Boies Penrose, a late 19th century Republican from Pennsylvania, told his business audience:

> "I believe in a division of labor. You send us to Congress; we pass the laws under which you make money...and out of your profits you further contribute to our campaign funds to send us back again to pass more laws to enable you to make more money." (*New York Times*, October 28, 1986)

Unfortunately, the crowd now in Washington are not so honest, or so eloquent, but are they doing anything different? Writing in the late 18th century, before capitalism thought it necessary to disguise its true character, Adam Smith, the "father" of bourgeois political economy, could state flatly:

> "Civil Government, so far as it is instituted for the security of property, is in reality instituted for the defense of the rich against the poor, or for those who have some property against those who have none at all."

Or as John Jay, one of our "Founding Fathers," put it in a sentiment that was shared by most of those who drew up the Constitution, "the people who own the country ought to govern it."

‡ Japan is a land of exam madness. Students take a big exam immediately on returning to school in September, and then four or five more before taking another big one in early summer. This happens every year until—after passing still another exam—they get into university. With success so dependent on scores in exams, a huge

industry of private cram schools has gotten started. Millions of students attend them every day after public school, and many families have gone heavily into debt to pay their huge fees. There are cram schools for all levels of education, even kindergarten, and because some cram schools have better track records than others there are also cram schools that prepare students to pass the exams that will gain them entrance into the better cram schools.

As you can imagine, most of these exams involve simple memorization. There is little thinking and less criticism, so it isn't surprising if the final result are millions of well disciplined, unimaginative, suicide prone whiz kids who are ready to excel at the next quiz show (which, not so incidentally, is the hottest item on Japanese T.V.). Lest you feel too superior to your Japanese peers on this score, you should know that the educational reforms (sic) picking up steam throughout the capitalist world are heading in just this direction. All this in the name of improving competitiveness. But against whom? Over what? Why? And isn't there an alternative, one more humane and also more conducive to real learning?

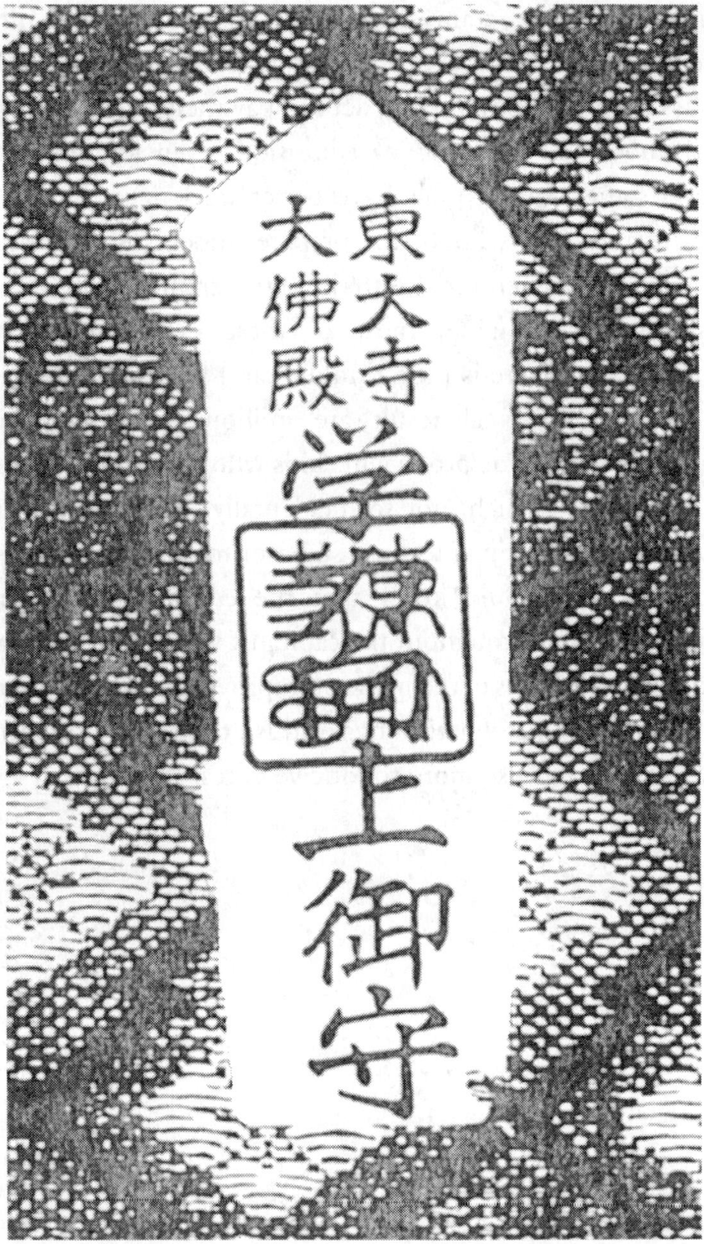

I bought this exam charm for you in a Buddhist temple in Kyoto—cost $5—just in case all my other advice fails to do you any good. In Japan, where exams are the national nightmare, *millions* of students carry this charm and others like it into their exams with them.

ELEVEN

The American social philosopher, Barrington Moore, says that:

> "To maintain and transmit a value system, human beings are punched, bullied, sent to jail, and thrown into concentration camps, cajoled, bribed, made into heroes, encouraged to read newspapers, stood up against a wall and shot, and sometimes even taught sociology."

Or economics, or psychology, or political science. What he neglects to mention is that the most effective of these is the last.

But don't think that most of the professors who maintain and transmit capitalist values—not, for the most part, by extolling the virtues of private enterprise but chiefly by taking capitalism for granted and ignoring the big questions—are comfortable in this task or are even fully aware of what they are doing. A 1964 poll of 500 political scientists, for example, showed that two out of three "agreed" or "strongly agreed" that much scholarship in the discipline is "superficial and trivial," and that concept formation and development is "little more than hair splitting and jargon." There is no reason to believe that the results today would be any different. There is a deep-going and on-going malaise among political scientists, and indeed professors throughout the academy, who are genuinely dissatisfied with what they do, but as long as they criticize their efforts as worthless (as indicated by the poll above) rather than conservative—it is worth a lot to our rulers—there is little chance that this will change.

‡ If an Oral Exam follows a written one, questions are likely to address: 1) whatever you've had trouble with in the written one (especially if already pointed out in the comments you've received); 2) people and books you've mentioned in asides; 3) particularly forceful positions you may have taken (along with the authors who hold contrary views); and 4) any idea dear to the hearts of the examiners, which often turns out to be something from their own work that relates to the questions you chose to write on.

For capitalism to work, it needs the help of the Government. The Government has four main functions in a capitalist society: 1) to help capitalists "accumulate capital" (expand their wealth through profitable investments); 2) to help capitalists "realize value" (sell what they produce—Government as Super-Salesman); 3) to repress and otherwise render ineffective all movements that threaten the social relations (mainly capitalist domination over workers) that underlay these developments; and 4) to legitimate all of the above in the eyes of the general public by masking its aims and the practices linked to them in the language of national interests, freedom, democracy, justice and patriotism.

Virtually everything our Government does can be placed under one or another of these headings, just because it is not really *our* Government but *their* Government, controlled by the capitalists and bent on serving their interests. This applies as much to foreign policy as to domestic policy. As more and more investment, lending and sales take place outside our national boundaries, American capitalists require the same kind of help from the Government around the globe that they have always received inside the country. "Imperialism" is the name given to this imperative—and it must be grasped as an imperative—and the sum of policies associated with it. One hundred and even fifty years ago, this usually took the form of militarily occupying foreign lands to ensure their total compliance with the needs of our capitalists.

More recently, in the stage of capitalism that has been dubbed "globalization," it has been found that the same goals could be attained just as effectively and with less opposition by using chains made of loans, investments, so-called aid (mostly to buy our products and to ensure a friendly military), and even culture. Convenient help in putting these chains in place is provided by such world (sic) organizations as the I.M.F., the World Bank and the W.T.O., all of which are dominated by the American Government, and, therefore, by American capital. In this strategy, it is very important that the rising middle class in these unfortunate lands come to mirror our own. Then, with all the parts in place, it no longer makes much difference if the man who calls himself President or Prime Minister is a local product or not. He cannot help but deliver what our capitalists want.

‡ What is it to be psychologically prepared for an exam? It may be easier to begin by listing those states to be avoided. You don't want to show up for an exam too tired, too anxious, too frightened; nor do you want to be too relaxed, too easy going and too casual. Instead, one should strive for a kind of creative tension where perceptual acuity and heightened concentration blend with the calm self-confidence of knowing that you are going to do well. You know you've got "it" when you can't wait for the exam to get started. As a rule, the mental and emotional conditions you are looking for can't be produced directly but are largely byproducts of what you've done in preparing for the exam. Thus, everything that goes into getting ready for the exam, including learning these exam hints, must also be judged in terms of how it affects your psychological state.

But why should our democratically elected Government do what the capitalists want? First, as indicated above, at the highest levels, our Government is made up of capitalists and their lawyers, and, at least in the U.S., this is true no matter which party is in power. Second, making a serious run for any major political office costs a small fortune, and capitalists are only willing to fund candidates who share their views (or who have no views and are simply willing to do what the capitalists want). Coverage in the capitalist owned media reflect the same set of priorities. Third—and this deserves more emphasis than it gets—given ours is a capitalist society in which the creation of both wealth and jobs is determined by the amount and direction of capitalist investment, the Government is forced to adopt policies that stimulate such investment. Since capitalists only invest in order to maximize profits, this third

reason translates into policies that help them produce more cheaply and in greater security, sell more easily, and reap the benefits of both in the culture. This is a structural constraint, in that the economy, being what it is, requires a certain kind of politics, no matter who is in power and no matter what their initial intentions, given that the Government is unwilling to overturn capitalism completely. Hence, the classic dilemma of social democracy, as evident from the recent histories of the

German Social Democratic, French Socialist, and British Labour Parties. In every case, these parties wished to have it both ways, that is, to keep an essentially capitalist economy while putting into effect a social program that favored workers' interests. In every case, the result was that the capitalists held back enough of their investment to harm the entire economy forcing the Social Democratic Government to reverse its pro-worker policies. The same reversal can be found in the recent history of Sweden, Spain, Australia, New Zealand, Jamaica and a dozen other countries.

While the capitalists retain the power to invest the surplus product of society, the margin for undertaking any policy that goes against their interests is very small. But one does not have to accept that society's wealth remain under the control of the capitalists. There are other ways to organize an economy, other rules to play by, other criteria that could determine investment decisions than maximizing the profit of a few. Just give your imagination a little room to maneuver, and you'll see them too.

‡ In Essay and Oral Exams, what constitutes good evidence varies somewhat with the discipline and with the school of thought to which one adheres. Still, how one marshals the evidence, how one organizes and presents it, and how one treats contrary evidence are always major components of a good answer. The last, in particular, shows the teacher that you're open to what you find that goes against your position as well as to what supports it. One of the marks of a good scholar.

Many of you are thinking, the courts, especially the Supreme Court, must be different. When William O. Douglas joined the Supreme Court just before World War II, then Chief Justice, Charles Evan Hughes, told him, "You must remember one thing. At the Constitutional level where we work, 90% of any decision is emotional. The rational part of us supplies the reason for supporting our predilections." So forget impartial justice, forget fairness. After some time on the Supreme Court, Douglas himself came to the conclusion that "The more the public learns about the inner workings of the Supreme Court...the harder it becomes to justify the special powers of this elite institution in our governmental scheme. And the justices know this." Hence, all the black robes, raised diases and legal mumbo-jumbo, only decipherable by a well paid priestly cast of lawyers. The Supreme Court is where the Wizard of Oz, with a wave of his Constitutional wand, tries to turn a land bleeding with capitalist excesses into a Walt Disney fairy tale about "the rule of law." The purpose of it all is not justice but legitimation. The bottom line is that whenever the Supreme Court speaks of "justice," they really mean "just-us."

‡ Walking out early from an exam. If your aim is to impress your fellow students (at least, those who won't hate you for upping their anxiety level), go ahead. The teacher is just as likely to think you don't know the answers, or that he/she made the exam too easy. But if you're interested in getting the best possible grade, don't waste these peak moments. Intellectually speaking, you're probably at your best during the last third of the exam. Re-reading the questions and your answers—there are always small errors to correct and things to add—will never fail to improve your performance.

The main problem confronting bourgeois ideology, is how to hide an elephant in the living room. The elephant, of course, is capitalism. Capitalism is no less conspicuous, and no less easy to disguise and defend, especially to an audience of people it is actively harming, than an elephant would be if it were roaming in your living room.

Left on its own, devoid of all rationalizations, capitalism is about as attractive as slavery and feudalism. That's why it's never left on its own. Instead, it is always accompanied by an elaborate set of ideas and concepts that Marx calls "bourgeois ideology." Some of this ideology simply reflects people's experience of living and working in capitalist society. After buying a number of things with money, for example, it's easy to get the idea that money—the thing, money viewed apart from all its social relations—has a mysterious power to obtain whatever its holder wants. This belief that something dead is really alive with its own special powers is what Marx calls "fetishism," and it plays an important role in his theory of alienation. But today, probably most ideology is the product of a huge consciousness industry that includes the media, the schools, advertising, mass spectator sports, the courts, the churches and much else. The chief aim of this consciousness industry is to convince us that capitalism is a good society, or—failing that—that it is the natural form of society (so that good or bad, nothing can be done about it), or—failing that—to so confuse us about who we are and what is happening to us that we can't even begin to think straight about the kind of society we live in and/or would like to live in.

These aims are achieved in three main ways: by hiding capitalism, by disguising it and by defending it. Hiding anything usually occurs by putting something else in front of it. Capitalism is too bulky for this to work, so bourgeois ideologists have found ways of hiding capitalism in plain sight. And the main technique they have used is calling it by another name. A German sociologist has counted 28 such names, the most important of which are "market society," "modern society," "post modern society," "globalization," "industrial society," "knowledge society," and "information society." Capitalists, too, as we saw earlier, prefer to go by other names in the popular press. The various substitutes for "capitalism" not only organize social reality in different ways, they also emphasize certain aspects of that reality just as they trivialize and/or ignore other aspects altogether.

An example of distorting capitalism is to view it as a result of individual choices, using as a model the purchases we make as consumers in the market. With this approach, all that influences individuals in making their choices just as the historical and structural restraints on the alternatives between which each individual must choose (in sum, all that Marxism emphasizes) is either trivialized or completely ignored. Rational Choice theory and methodological individualism more generally are the main vehicles for this approach in the academy. An example of defending capitalism is arguing that capitalism is a necessary precondition for freedom and democracy. (It is. That is, it is for "capitalist" freedom and "capitalist" democracy, and we have seen what they are like.) Hiding capitalism, distorting it and defending it are often found together, but it is important to separate them out if only to see that it is the first activity that is decisive. Capitalism is not very easy to disguise or defend, especially when the problems associated with it have noticeably worsened. But, as with the elephant, if you can hide capitalism, there is no need to disguise or defend it. Hence, the main efforts of bourgeois ideology—and now more than ever—has gone into hiding capitalism.

What exactly is it about capitalism that our rulers are trying to hide? The short list would have to include: 1) that the most apt label for our society—because it brings into focus how our society works (particularly in production, an area of life that most of the other labels ignore or obscure), for whom it works better, for whom it works worse, and its potential for change—is "capitalism"; 2) that the real rulers of this society are those who own the means of production, distribution and exchange, and reap the bulk of the surplus; 3) that the Government, whatever democratic foreplay goes on, serves their interests, hence is their Government and not ours; 4) that we, the rest of us who don't live on profit, rent or interest, are workers (whether we are willing to admit it or not), because we are forced to seek work in order to live; 5) that the conditions of life and work for us workers are bad and likely to get much worse—while the wealth of the capitalists keeps growing; 6) that a qualitatively better life, a more humane, just, free, democratic, egalitarian and ecologically rational way of organizing society can be developed; 7) that those who benefit from the present order of society have consistently lied to us about all of the above; and

8) that once workers—in the broad sense of the term—break through these lies and half-truths, they/we can win.

Now the best way for the capitalists to hide all of these facts is to hide the first one, that our's is a capitalist society, because once people learn this all of the facts that follow become easier to see and to grasp. In his book, *In Praise of Folly*, Erasmus tells the story of a man watching a play who all at once jumps onto the stage and tears the masks off of the actors to reveal who they really are. If you think of Marx as this man and the capitalists as the actors, you can begin to understand both what Marx does and why the capitalists are not too pleased with him for doing it.

‡ Where to sit for the exam. "You've got to be kidding." I'm not. It makes only a marginal difference, but often that's all it takes to make winners out of losers in exams as in Black Jack and, indeed, throughout life. If you sit close to the teacher, you will probably get to see the exam first and hand it in last, which could add up to a minute to your writing time. People to avoid sitting next to, if you can help it, include your best friend (whose anxious looks and other vibrations you don't need at this moment), the class whiz (whose constant writing when you're still trying to figure something out may depress you), and the kid who keeps jiggling one of his legs (for obvious reasons). Also, stay away from the door or windows if there is noise coming from either.

It was Plato, not Marx, who first said, "A city is always composed of at least two parts, which are at war with one another—the rich and the poor." In this war, the poor have numbers, while the rich have money, money to buy instruments of force but also means to influence the thinking of the poor. For the longest time, this was the popular wisdom. Even today, people who study slave societies have no difficulty grasping the decisive role played by the division between slaves and slave owners. Feudalism, too, is generally interpreted along lines of the cleavage between serfs and feudal lords. In both cases, it is the conflict between those who produce food, clothing, etc., and those who control the means by which production takes place that conditions major political and cultural developments in these societies.

Then, in capitalism, something happens, not to society, but to the ability and/or willingness of most people to view society in the above manner. Capitalism, too, has people—now called "workers"—who produce the goods we all use; and there is another, much smaller group who own and control the means, now chiefly machines, factories and offices, that are used in the production and distribution of these goods. These are the capitalists. The clash between these two classes over jobs, wages, conditions of work, etc.—and the institutional power to decide on such matters—is at the core of what is meant by "class struggle."

According to Marx, history—that is the recorded history of our species—is largely the history of class struggle, especially in its interaction with changes in the mode of production (or in how wealth gets produced, distributed and exchanged). Trying to make sense of the society into which we are born without learning this history is a lot like entering a theater in the middle of a movie and trying to understand the plot without knowing what happened before we got there. Who would want to see a movie in this way? Yet, the a-historical bent of most of our contemporaries allows them to treat society in a way that they would never treat a film. The evolving class struggles of earlier times, however, that have structured and colored every important aspect of our society, cannot be neglected if we are to make adequate sense of both the present and its possible future.

There is also a major political advantage of organizing thinking around the notion of "class struggle," in what is called "class analysis," in that it helps workers link up what they are suffering from with who is responsible for it, which groups have an interest in change, and how the latter can be brought together. The capitalists' entire power and all their privileges depend on keeping the more numerous workers from making these connections, which is why the media and schools controlled by the wealthy have put a virtual embargo on the notion of "class struggle" and what accounts for the outlaw status of this idea in our culture. When is the last time, for example, one of *your* professors mentioned the class struggle?

A frequent criticism heard from the Pope and other conservatives is that class struggle is an invention of the Left. Not So! says ex-priest and president of Haiti, Jean Bertrand Aristide: "I did not invent class struggle, no more than Karl Marx did. Perhaps the idea that one invents class struggle is possible if one never leaves the squares of the Vatican or the heights of Petionville [a wealthy suburb in Port-au-Prince]. But who can avoid encountering class struggle in the heart of Port-au-Prince? It is not a subject of controversy, but a fact, a given."

‡ Why study regularly? You expect me to say that this is the best way to do well on exams. Of course, it is. But that's obvious. I want to make another kind of pitch for keeping up with your course assignments. It makes learning the pleasure it can be. A student who is up to date on his work experiences life differently. He enjoys his reading more and gets more out of it, because he is not rushed. He has the time to contextualize the subject, to see how it is related to what else he knows and to what is happening in society. He is not anxious about appearing dumb in class, and can get more out of lectures. He is less worried about exams. He is also more comfortable with teachers, even those with whom he disagrees, and can question them with authority. Through all this, he ("she," too, of course) transforms the teacher from a high school teacher and exam coach into a university professor, and reaps the corresponding intellectual rewards.

Why study regularly? Because you want an education from your education, because learning should fill you with excitement and not fear and anxiety (and developing a critical slant on what you learn can bring you the greatest excitement of all), and—yes, of course—because this is the surest way to a higher grade. So give it a try, even if it's only in one course, and discover for yourself the enormous difference that studying regularly can make to your whole life as a student.

TWELVE

Marx is the only one of our great political thinkers who didn't write for everyone. Of course, everyone can read him, and there is something important that everyone can learn from his writings. But at the core of his message is the idea that people have different interests, objective interests, that derive from their relationship to the prevailing mode of production (how most wealth gets produced in capitalism), and that it is in the interests of the workers to listen carefully to what he has to say, to make the connections needed to understand him, and to act upon his words once they are understood; just as it is in the interests of capitalists, those who buy labor power in order to put capital into motion, not to listen, and to distort and deny what Marx is saying.

Class interests includes all that it makes sense for people to do and to believe, given the benefits these bring them in the particular situation of their class. For the capitalists, this translates into all that makes them higher profits and secures their ability to continue making such profits in the future. Marx's writings are rightly seen as threatening these interests. While the workers' main interests lie in winning higher wages, shorter hours, safer and more secure jobs, and in creating the conditions necessary—including structural changes in society—for these goals to be reached for all workers and over the long term. The incompatibility between the class interests of the workers and capitalists is the basis of the ongoing class struggle between these two groups.

It is evident that not all workers and capitalists grasp their class interests, though I think most capitalists do. To grasp their class interests, workers have to overcome a large number of barriers placed in their way both by life in capitalism and by the consistently biased interpretations of this life by schools, media, churches, etc. Yet, with the help of their necessary cooperation on the job and the fact that they are all subjected to the same exploitation by the boss (something that becomes increasingly evident in bad times through wage reductions, speed-ups, lay-offs, etc.), most workers gradually become conscious of at least some of their class interests. Marx writes as much to affect this situation as to describe and explain it—hence, he addresses himself essentially to workers (in the broadest sense of this term)—because only when a majority of the workers become conscious of their interests (or "class conscious") does humanity, including capitalists, have a chance to advance from capitalism into socialism.

As human beings, everyone would benefit from socialism. Therefore, it is in everyone's human interest to replace capitalism with socialism. There is also a lot that occurs in capitalism, like the wanton destruction of the environment, that is against everybody's human interests. But if this is so, why doesn't Marx give human interests the same weight as class interests in making his case for socialism? Why doesn't he appeal to capitalists, in their capacity as human beings, as well as to workers? The answer is that, unless one is actually living in Love Canal or its equivalent (and even then), human interests do not exert the same pressure that class interests do on either people's thinking or behavior. (The possible exception is young people, particularly students.) If it did, the major religions, all of which appeal to a version of human interests, would have turned our society into a heaven on earth long ago.

As the bridge over which the workers must pass in moving from their conditions of life and work to revolutionary praxis, class interests is constantly under ideological bombardment by the capitalist class, and just as constantly being fixed and rebuilt by socialists. Helping workers attain consciousness of their class interests, while capitalists and their paid fighters are doing all that they can to block it, is what most socialist political activity is all about.

‡ When the first I.Q. tests were given to Australian Aborigines, they registered as low grade morons. Here, it was not only the cultural biases reflected in the questions that were at fault but also the fact that each student had to answer the questions by him/herself. In Aboriginal society, all important problem solving is done collectively, so as soon as a student was given the test he wanted to consult with his friends. The examiners could only understand this as an attempt to cheat, and they refused to let the students talk to one another.

In our society, we do a certain amount of problem solving individually, and a certain amount collectively, in cooperation with others who are experiencing the same or similar problems. By placing us in a situation where each person must answer all questions by himself, exams appear to deny this cooperative dimension to our thinking. Disconnected and isolated from others in this way, we may be a little easier for *them* to evaluate, but we are certainly a lot easier for *them* to control.

"Know Thyself" sums up a big part of the wisdom that comes to us from many different schools of philosophy. But which self, for we all have a number of different identities—racial, gender, national, religious, species, class and others—each with its own set of interests and each of great importance for dealing with one or another problem? The key question then becomes how to focus on the identity (on that part of who and what we are) that is most relevant to the problem at hand? The priority that Marxists give to our identity as members of a class is not due to an idealization of workers, or any belief that workers suffer more than Blacks or women or any other oppressed group, but to the particular nature of the problems (this book is full of them) that Marxists are trying to understand and resolve.

To avoid possible misunderstanding, I should emphasize that I am fully aware that there have been important changes in recent years in the structure of work and in the nature of the work force; that up to this point in U.S. history, class based politics have not been very successful; that most workers have not shown much interest in it; that trade unions never lived up to the promise evident in their earlier heroic period; that the more successful social movements on the Left today are organized around racial, gender and environmental issues; and that some of the labor and socialist groups, that do emphasize class, have not been sufficiently sensitive to other kinds of oppression. All this is true, but it doesn't affect my main argument: that capitalism, which is responsible for most of our suffering, is nearing the end of its tether, that working people of all kinds have the greatest interest in getting rid of capitalism, and that they alone have the power—which comes from their numbers and their place in the economic system—to do so and to put something far better in its place. As far as politics is concerned, this means placing one's identity as a worker up front, and giving priority to organizing around the interests people have as workers.

‡ It is said that, "Facing a firing squad concentrates the mind wonderfully." In Studying for an Exam, we cannot count—thank goodness—on that kind of help. Instead, we must bring ourselves to attention. Such attention is one part will power, two parts emotional state, and three parts a function of the interest a particular subject holds for you. Unfortunately, at the point when you are studying for an exam, it is too late to decide that you have no interest in the course, or, probably, to generate an interest that is not there. The only things that you can affect are your emotional state and your will.

What's called "will power" is often nothing more than refusing to allow either your fundamental beliefs or your emotional state to determine your behavior in what is essentially a strategic situation. The aim in taking an exam is to do well, something you're already committed to in virtue of having come so far in the course. In short, this is no time to complain how bad the course or the teacher is. That should have come earlier, and, of course, there will be lots of time for that later. Now, you are in the position of a general drawing up a battle plan in order to win the war. *Atten-tion*!

SNAKE OILS

How do you keep people from seeing the injustices and irrationality of our capitalist society that stares them in the face every day of their lives? It's snake oil that does it. Here's my short list of the most commonly used snake oils. How many of these have you taken lately?

1) Trivializing: "It's not as bad as it seems."
2) Mislabeling: Killing becomes "collateral damage"
3) Disconnecting: Treating poverty, unemployment, malnutrition, etc., as if they were separate problems.
4) Minimizing: "Only 25% are going hungry."
5) Polyanaizing: "That means 75% have enough to eat."
6) Erasing social ties: "Think only of yourself. No one is thinking about you."
7) Blaming the victim: "If they only tried harder, and had more self-control, and more patience, and..."
8) Blaming human nature: "That's what people are like."
9) Routinizing: "They're used to sleeping outdoors at night."
10) Naturalizing: "It always been like that."
11) Holocausting: "This may be bad, but compared to the destruction of the Jews (or that caused by World War II, or starvation in Somalia, etc.) it's not very serious."

12) Means/Ends Rationalizing: "To make an omelet, you've got to break some eggs."

13) Overgeneralizing: Flattening out the specifics that enable us to see it and treat it, i.e., substituting "ruling elite" for "capitalist class," or "oppression" for "exploitation."

14) Futilizing: "Nothing can be done in any case."

15) Stalling: "We need to set up another committee to study the problem."

16) Forgetting: Watch T.V., go to a rock concert, play ball.

17) Window shopping: Buy, buy, buy, or at least fantasize about it. Window shopping is the number one past-time of teen-age girls in America. And, at least, this way you don't see who is sleeping on the sidewalk just behind you.

18) Projecting an image of care: "We gave at the office."

19) Passing the buck: "Don't we have an agency to take care of that?"

20) Leaving it to Superman: Eli Weisel (or Pope John Paul, or Michael Jackson) is at work on it."

21) Blaming the messenger: "Damn it, Ollman. Why did you have to tell us about these things?"

So be practical, be macho (hide your feelings), go along to get along, keep your feet on the ground, your nose to the grindstone, your head in the sand. Show impatience only for what deserves understanding, and limitless tolerance for what should receive a blow from your hammer. Be patriotic, love your country as it is, with all its warts, taking pride in the constant patter to do away with them. Keep hope alive. Have a nice day, and don't forget to swallow your daily dose of snake oils. What, me worry?

Well, that's one possible reaction. This book offers you another.

‡ At the start of this book, I sought to assuage the guilt people feel for most of the bad things that have happened to them. I said, "It's not

your fault." Tests, on the other hand, are society's main way of telling you otherwise. So that when you can't find a job, or have one that is boring and poorly paid, or when you can't find a home you can afford, and so on, you end up blaming yourself. Just like in school, you think, you didn't get the grade you wanted because you didn't try hard enough, or you simply don't have what it takes. It's you and what you are or have done (or haven't done) that is responsible. Hence, it is you who is guilty. The several hundred, if not thousands, of exams, tests and quizzes you've taken since you started school have had their effect. But what if—as I've argued throughout this book—the deck is stacked against you? There is no more important service that all these tests perform for our ruling class than getting you to mistake a hostile social environment for a personal defect.

A recent study of seventeen-year-olds found that 47% of them believed that the words "from each according to his ability, to each according to his needs" came from the U.S. Constitution and not—as is the case—from the *Communist Manifesto*. Poor education, as some conservatives were quick to suggest? Or a sign of a widespread commitment to social justice together with the naive belief that any idea that makes so much sense must be part of our foundational document? Don't underestimate young people's strong drive for justice before all the mis-education they receive obfuscates (temporarily?) what it really means...and requires.

WHEREVER YOU FIND INJUSTICE, THE PROPER FORM OF POLITENESS IS ATTACK.
T-BONE SLIM
KONOPACKI
OR THE KERR CO.

THIRTEEN

The American humorist, James Thurber, tells the story of a friend who asked him, "How is your wife." Thurber replied, "Compared to what?" Yes, I know I already used this story in discussing exams earlier, but it contains an equally important lesson for dealing with society. Most of the judgements we make in life involve comparisons of one sort or another, but it isn't always obvious what the relevant object of comparison is. Yet, the comparison chosen, and this is often done unconsciously or out of habit with no thought given to alternatives, will have a decisive effect on the judgement made.

What, then, is the relevant object of comparison in judging our society? It is not, as so many defenders of the *status quo* insist, some other country with a very different history and conditions. Given these differences, they couldn't be like us if they wanted to, nor we like them. Hence, it is monumentally irrelevant to respond to criticism of the U.S. by saying: "Well, you're eating better than you would in India," or "You are freer than you would be in North Korea." With our particular history and conditions, however, the U.S. has the potential for being something more, something much better than it is. In the same way that one judges the performance of an athlete by what he/she is capable of, one should judge each society by what it could be, given all that it has going for it. This is also the only truly relevant standard for making judgements in any area of life. Well, using what our wealth, industry, skills, education, democratic traditions, etc. make possible as our object of comparison, can you really be satisfied with the present state of our country?

‡ The list of ways in which exams prepare students for life in our capitalist society is longer still:

1) By fixing a time and a form in which they have to deliver or else, exams prepare students for the more rigorous discipline of the work situation that lies ahead;

2) In forcing students to think and write faster than they ordinarily do, it gets them ready—mentally, emotionally and also morally—for the speed-ups they will face on the job;

3)The self-discipline students acquire in preparing for exams also helps them put up with the disrespect, personal abuse and boredom that awaits them at work;

4) Exams are orders that are not open to question—"discuss this," "outline that," etc.—and taking so many exams conditions one to accept unthinkingly the orders that will come from their future employers;

5) By fitting the infinite variety of answers given on exams into the straitjackets of A,B,C,D and F, students get accustomed to the impersonal job categories that will constitute such an important part of their identity later on;

6) Because of the superior knowledge of the teacher, students tend to assume that those who are above them in other hierarchies—at work or in politics—also know more than they do;

7) Because most teachers are genuinely concerned with the well being of their students, many students also assume, incorrectly, that those who stand in a similar relation to them in other hierarchies must feel the same;

8) With the Damocles sword of a failing grade hanging over their heads throughout their years in school, the inhibiting fear of swift

and dire punishment never leaves students, no matter what their later situation;

9) Because there is always so much students don't know, exams—especially so many of them—tend to raise students' level of anxiety and to undermine their self-confidence, with the result that most of them remain unsure they will ever know enough to criticize existing institutions, and even physically uncomfortable at the thought of putting something better in their place. Is it any wonder that life itself is often experienced as a series of exams for which one is never quite prepared, never quite in time, and never quite finished? For confirming evidence, check your dreams.

Exams? They are the chain that binds students to their desks and to the *status quo*, the treadmill that prepares them for the still bigger rat race to come, the gun at the head that threatens to go off should they try to move away, and, maybe worst of all, the drug that so befogs students' minds that they take this mad scene for normal.

If a man has lost his legs, that should be enough of an explanation for why he can't run. What more does it add to say that his technique is faulty or that he has the wrong attitude? Similarly, after admitting that none of the material conditions Marx considered essential for building socialism were present in Russia in 1917 or in China in 1949, what more does it add to say that the regimes that came to power in those countries followed faulty economic or political strategies, or that their subsequent experience shows that socialism can't work? In the case of our legless man, this shifts most of the blame onto him. Similarly, in the case of Russia and China, this shifts most of the blame for their failure on to their political leaders and/or the very idea of socialism. In short, it is one thing to mention the impossible situation in which these regimes began (most writers do, if only briefly); it is another to draw the logical consequences of such an admission (most don't).

While the so-called "socialist countries" were not in any position to build socialism, this does not mean they did not ameliorate the material existence of most of their citizens (something that the people of Eastern Europe are increasingly willing to admit). Nor does it follow from the fact that capitalist conditions did succeed in accumulating wealth in western Europe and a few other countries that it could do so everywhere. My remarks on the absence of socialism in the so-called "socialist countries," therefore, should not be taken as a rejection of all these countries achieved, or as a back-handed endorsement of the capitalist road to development, with all its horrors and its own inconclusive results. Rather, my focus here, as throughout this book, is on what capitalism is and what we can do with the means it itself has made available to resolve the problems that have arisen in its wake. It is only in this context, and at this moment, that socialism becomes a real possibility.

"They're going to make slaves of the Russian people." (Good Morning, 1921)

‡ Studying in a Group requires that you structure your session very carefully. The group has two basic aims: to improve its members' understanding of difficult problems and texts, and to develop each person's ability to translate what he/she knows into good answers to exam questions. While both aims deserve attention, my main concern here has been with the latter, and many of these exam hints can be incorporated into your group sessions.

Working through old exam questions—not so much to answer them as to indicate possible approaches—is a particularly effective way of studying with other people. For Oral Exams, the study group should adopt the role of the examining committee and each student should take turns passing through the gauntlet of the "committee's" questions. Look at my earlier comments on oral exams to develop a realistic set of questions. The more practice you get at this, the more comfortable and—probably—the more effective you'll be when faced with the real thing.

What, then, would socialism, our socialism, look like? Marx believes that in socialism you will help make the decisions now made by the president and board of trustees of your university, by the boss on your job, by your landlord, by the owners of newspapers, T.V. stations, movie studios, and sports franchises, and by government officials at all levels. Extending democracy, the rule of the people, into all areas of society is the key difference that marks this period. It is the socialist alternative to the dictatorship of money, and of those who have most of it, that characterizes life in capitalist society. And everywhere, the aim of maximizing profit for the few will be replaced by the human aim of serving social needs.

In the economy, this doesn't only mean making more of the things people really need—which in our wealthy country could eliminate poverty in a few years—but making them better and distributing them more fairly, while showing equal concern for preserving the environment, protecting the health of workers and consumers, and reducing hours of work (all important "social needs"). This is possible because all the factors of production available to society will be put to full use. There will be no idle machines, wasted raw materials, and, above all, no unemployed workers. Recall the $15 trillion spent on arms since World War II, the waste in what gets made and in what doesn't, the conspicuous baubles of the rich, and all the money spent on repression and on brainwashing us from thinking about just these kinds of questions—view all this in light of the rapid advances being made in automation, computerization and robotization—and then tell me it can't be done.

The institutional forms of democracy that will enable people to participate in making decisions on all such matters range from self-management committees at workplaces, schools, and home communities, to city and regional councils, to national and world governments, to a central planning and coordinating board, whose members will be elected by everyone and whose priorities will be set after general debate and on the basis of majority rule.

Though some small businesses will remain privately owned at the start of socialism, the goal is to achieve full public ownership of the means of production, distribution and exchange, and of the social means of consumption (parks, theaters, rail roads, etc.)—but *not* the private means of consumption (cars, clothes, homes, etc.)—as soon as possible. With the abolition of inheritance for everything but personal effects, even small capitalists won't be able to leave their businesses to their children, who will have to find real jobs like everyone else.

On the job, wage differentials, though greatly reduced, will continue to exist as long as there are some people who require this kind of incentive to do their best. Over time, as other incentives—pride in a job well done, praise of one's co-workers, satisfaction in serving the community, etc.—replace the desire to get rich and the fear of being poor (since there are no longer rich or poor), wages will tend to be the same for everyone who works the same number of hours. These wages will be more than enough to buy what people want, since many of the things that cost so much today will be free—such as education, including college and other kinds of special training, health care and, probably very quickly, transportation, communication and entertainment—and others will be heavily subsidized, such as housing and basic items of food and clothing. Also, with production determined by democratic social planning rather than by individuals seeking to maximize their profits, and a growing number of the things we use apportioned by need rather than cost, the role of money in society (money as we know it) will gradually diminish, and with it the grip of money on our psyches.

Throughout socialist society, in education but also at work and at play, special efforts will be made to counter selfishness and the fear of what is different, and to promote the values of cooperation and mutual concern. With people participating in making the key decisions that effect their varied activities, products and social relations, alienation—with its accompanying feelings of disconnectedness and powerlessness—will gradually give way to feelings of empowerment and a deep sense of belonging to a single human community. In the process, freedom, equality and democracy, all the noble ideals that capitalism (to its credit) first set out, and then (to its shame) proceeded to undermine and distort, will finally become actual descriptions of our life together in society.

It should be evident that socialism, as outlined here, cannot work if there is very little to share, but if material abundance already exists and is simply badly distributed, it can. Socialism can't work if industrialization hasn't yet taken place, but where it has, it can. Socialism can't work if complex organizations for the production and distribution of goods haven't already been set up, but where they have, it can. Socialism can't work if society is divided up into many different classes with distinct and competing interests, but in a society where most people have become wage and salary earners and have the same basic interests, it can. Socialism can't work where there is no democracy, but where there is and people choose to expand its field of operations to include the whole of society, it can. In the latter set of conditions, not only can socialism work, but nothing can work as well. And all the experiences of countries where these conditions never existed—the Soviet Union, China, etc.—are simply and thoroughly irrelevant as far as teaching us about what we could do here and now. That the media puts these negative experiences at the center of all their discussions of socialism is but a reminder of who owns the media and their interests in confusing and misleading the rest of us over the real possibilities that make up our future.

Granted that existing conditions make socialism a real possibility, one might still ask: why would the workers use these conditions in just this way? The answer is that every ruling class throughout history has tried to build a society in line with its class interests, so why think that workers, once they become the ruling class, will do anything else? The workers main class interest at this time is to abolish the conditions that underlie their exploitation, and the various measures described above all serve this end.

‡ An alternative to the typical exam, where each individual is thrown into a deadly competition with others, is the COOPERATIVE EXAM, where students work together to produce a common product. Virtually any number can "play." Probably the high point of the exercise occurs at the very beginning when the participants suggest different questions for study, and debate their respective merits. In choosing one or two to work on and dividing among themselves areas for further investigation, students can acquire as good an overview of the subject as any the teacher might provide.

After completing their research projects, one student tries to stitch together what the others have found or concluded. Then, the entire group meets to discuss and modify the result. Finally, the teacher gets to read or listen to what the students have done, and to react to it, after which it is again the students' turn to ask questions, disagree and the like. The grade, when it comes, is for the entire project from the initial choice of questions to how students responded to criticisms, and everyone who contributed to it in any way receives the same grade. We could, of course, dispense with the grade completely. At this point, who needs it? Not the students. Unfortunately, in the system in which we are operating, this is not possible (I know—I tried it once, and got slapped down by the Dean's Office).

There is no question but that the process described here assumes a certain sense of responsibility and a high degree of cooperation on the part of the students, but it also helps to develop just these qualities, to say nothing of the self-confidence that comes from bypassing the authority of the teacher. When education is more concerned with helping students realize their potential as human beings and less so with producing the knowledge, skills and attitudes that best serve the interests of a ruling class, we can expect a lot more cooperative exams. Until then, it might be worthwhile to try one just to see what you're missing.

George Bernard Shaw defines "barbarian" as "someone who takes the morality of his own country as human nature." Are you one of Shaw's "barbarians?" There is probably nothing about which people feel more certain, yet know less, than human nature, or what human beings are really like. So I suppose it is understandable that the most frequent criticism I hear from students and others about socialism is that people are too selfish, too competitive, too uncaring, too full of fears and hatreds to live in a society that requires such a high degree of cooperation. Hence, socialism, it is often said, though a nice idea, couldn't work. Nor do those who raise this objection lack evidence, since we all know a lot of people—possibly even ourselves—who exhibit some of these negative qualities. It should be obvious, though, that the entire sample used here is but a minute fraction of the earth's population, and it is all drawn from one society, our own, and probably from only one or two groups in that society. If, however, we look at all the societies we know something about, "primitive" as well as advanced, past as well as present, the range of what is done, believed, wanted, feared, hoped for, etc. is enormous. From all this, it is impossible to single out any traits—whether good or bad—as indicative of basic human nature. All that stands out from this body of evidence is the great variety of ways associated with being human and the extraordinary flexibility our species possesses for adapting itself to very different conditions.

Those who criticize socialism on the grounds of human nature, like Shaw's "barbarian," have simply mistaken what most people have been made into by life in our capitalist society for human nature as such. Socialists, on the other hand, believe that in a society where people are permitted, encouraged, aided and abetted, praised and even rewarded for cooperating and showing mutual concern everyone (but particularly the young) will gradually develop these qualities as part of their human nature. It should be clear that I am not claiming that people are naturally good, or loving, or cooperative. That is still another view, and no doubt some socialists subscribe to it, though I associate it more with anarchism. The Marxist position, to which I hold, is that by nature people are neither good or bad but have potential for both, as well as for everything in between, and that the mixture of character traits they actually develop are those made possible, functional, practical, desirable and sometimes even necessary by their particular society and the class to which they belong in that society. It is this view that best explains the evidence of human behavior from the present and the past. Why shouldn't it explain what is likely to occur in the future under the unique conditions that come into being in socialism?

The Italian communist philosopher, Antonio Gramsci, said that the question, "What is Man?" (probably the most important question in philosophy) is really the question, "What can man become?" The full answer, of course, is still unknown, but history, sociology and anthropology are full of evidence that some conditions do a much better job than others in helping people realize their potential for cooperation, mutual concern and creativity. The whole socialist project can be summed up as an attempt to contribute to the conditions that would permit the full unfolding of this potential.

‡ Who gives you exams outside of school? I mean, who else grills you besides your teachers, and what do they want from you? Well, there's the potential employer, who wants to know if you will make a suitable employee; the police, who are trying to find out if you've broken the law; there's the I.R.S. (income tax) and customs, who want to know how much money you owe them; the welfare, housing and unemployment agencies, who are trying to determine if you deserve their help, or, if you are already getting help, following their rules; the opinion polls, who are informing candidates for political office what opinions they should pretend to have; and salesmen and advertisers of various sorts, who are looking for an angle so they can sell you something. It is clear that these tests at least have nothing to do with education and everything to do with control and the desire on the part of those who administer the tests to shape your behavior in ways that suit their interests. Is there a message for you in all this?

In about 1800 B.C., a Sumerian father wrote to his son, "Go to school, stand before your teacher, recite your assignment...Be humble and show fear before your superiors." Back then, I don't think people had much difficulty seeing the connection.

Communism is a later and higher stage of socialism. When the transition from capitalism has been completed, which is something that may take a century or more, the economic, social and political foundations laid by socialism will open the way to a new, qualitatively superior way of life. With communism, the period of human history characterized by various forms of alienation comes to an end. The various elements of what it means to be a human being in terms of essential activities, products and social relations that had been separated from one another, mystified and placed under hostile alien control are finally reunited and brought under the collective control of the workers themselves, which at this time includes everybody. In the process, a thorough-going cooperation and mutual concern have replaced selfish competition and mutual neglect. Social interaction has lost its instrumental character, and people relate to each other for the sake of the other and the sheer pleasure of doing things together. Scarcity in all basic goods has been abolished, and wealth is now understood not as a collection of objects—which are there for the asking in any case—but as the expansion of free time. People are now free to become everything they can be, and helped by society (which means by each other) to do so; and this positive freedom is enjoyed by everyone. Unfolding the full creative potential inherent in the human species is the exciting adventure that awaits those lucky enough to live in this period.

Communism is a lot like sex. No one has to advocate it. It is generally enough to cut through the capitalist inspired mystification that surrounds communism for most people to recognize that it is in their deepest human interest. For communism, after all, combines the highest ideals of the philosophers and the moral teachings of all major religions with the material achievements of capitalism and the social advances made under socialism. It is the blessings of all earlier religious and ethical systems, multiplied many fold, realized in the here and now.

Does this sound like a bit much? You may be right. That's why it is important to treat communism not as a finished form of society but as the direction in which socialism, which is relatively easy to conceive, would evolve. Our descendants will have the enviable task of determining just how far down this road the human species can travel.

‡ Exams and sexual repression are the two main ways we socialize the young. In both cases, it is the whole of society that jumps on the backs of young people and stays there until the free flow of emotions assumes a socially acceptable form and their will echoes the will of their trainers. The first goal is attained by repressing their strongest

feelings, and the second—far more than is recognized—by overwhelming them with an endless series of exams that masquerades as education. The reordered emotions then interact with their captured volition to forge a personality in which one's true self is held prisoner.

Breaking out of this jail requires that we know something about the material out of which it is constructed, but also how it functions, who built it, and why. What else is this but a kind of street smarts for life in the biggest and most dangerous neighborhood of all, global capitalism? Only with the appropriate street smarts can students make the judgements and develop the strategies necessary to reclaim their freedom. Without a grasp of such basic matters, rebellion is not a free act, just a stubborn one, and what passes for rebellion is often very self-destructive. Taking drugs, engaging in unsafe sex, or refusing to take or prepare for a scheduled exam are not free acts, because they don't take full account of the context or of the effect of one's action. Freedom is not simply doing what you want, but includes knowing how to do it, when to do it, why you should do it, and, sometimes, why you shouldn't.

FOURTEEN

So "Is it time," as the conservative writer, William Buckley, asks (*New York Daily News*, December 12, 1980), "to bury Karl Marx?" Well, it all depends on the position one takes on Cacus. Cacus was a Roman mythological figure, half man—half beast, who stole oxen by dragging them backwards into his cave, so that their footprints made it appear that they had gone out from there. After quoting Luther's account of this story, Marx exclaims, "An excellent picture, it fits the capitalist in general, who pretends that what he has taken from others and brought back to his den emanates from him, and by causing it to go backwards, he gives it the semblance of having come from his den."

Capitalists present themselves as producers of wealth, providers of jobs, donors and public benefactors. A quick examination of their activities would make it appear that nothing and no one gets going without their okaying it. These are the "footprints" in the sand, and they are there for all to see. From them, it is easy to conclude that anything the capitalists manage to retain for themselves as profit is their just and well-earned reward.

But, as in the case of Cacus, this does not tell the whole story. To find out what happened to the oxen, we would have to go back to the night before (to do a little history) and poke our heads into the cave (examine the larger context). The full truth, when we discover it, is the exact opposite of the apparent truth. In the case of the capitalists, only by investigating how most businessmen have obtained their wealth from the surplus labor of previous generations of workers (history), and how the laws and customs of our society are biased in their favor (the larger context), can we see that it is not the capitalists who are serving society (and, hence, deserving a reward), but the rest of society that is serving them. The businessman's power to make important decisions is not denied—the "footprints" are there—but, by placing the exercise of this power within its social and historical contexts, what it all means gets turned around.

In their different ways, all of Marx's theories perform this common work. So long as capitalism hides its real relations behind its appearances, its underlying processes behind its surface events, class struggle behind class collaboration, and its potential for an egalitarian order behind the present in-egalitarian one—so long will Marxism be needed to uncover the true situation. And the capitalists and their "intellectual handmaidens" who insist that "it's time to bury Karl Marx." Well, Cacus, too, had an interest in keeping people from finding out what went on in his cave.

‡ In Reading, Note-taking and Studying for an exam, always try to connect what you're learning to the "big picture," the key storyline, the central problem or main theory or debate of which it is a part. This should give you a basis for classifying and judging as well as prioritizing most of this material, and will help immeasurably in organizing your answers for most essay and oral exams. It is also the secret for memorizing what you've learned over the long run.

A Zen Buddhist monk appeared before his students one day with a large stick and announced that he was going to ask them a question. If a student didn't know the answer, the monk said, he would hit him with the stick. And if the student knew the answer, well, he would also get hit with the stick. Got it? The monk then asked his question and raised his stick. What were the students to do? Was there any way to avoid getting hit? After several students said "Yes" and got hit, and a few others answered "No" and got hit, one student had the bright idea of grabbing the stick. That was the only way out, and it worked.

In the United States we face a similar dilemma. In politics, we are given a choice whether to vote for the Democrats or the Republicans, but no matter which party wins, we lose. Changing our vote from one party to the other and back again, as so many have done, doesn't keep us from getting hit, with all the disappointment that routinely ensues. The point is that the choice we are given is a false one. There is no possibility of solving any of our major problems if we allow their solutions to be posed in this way. But how can we grab this particular stick?

‡ In Oral Exams, it is sometimes possible to end your answer with a question or otherwise provoke your examiners to tell you what they think of what has just been asked. Your professors are really suffering from having to remain silent for so long, and most of them wouldn't mind giving you one final "lesson." If, from there, you can get your examiners to argue among themselves, it is a sign they've already started to treat you as a peer. A mark of a first class, and enjoyable, examination.

Revolution: first, what it isn't. It isn't simply a change in Government; nor is it every violent and unconstitutional means used to bring about such a change; nor is it something that occurs in a day or even a year. Like the etymology of the word suggests, revolution is a full turn of the wheel. It is a total transformation in the economic, social and political life of a society, and it brings this about by replacing the class currently in power with another class that has different interests and other ways of putting them into practice. If the democratic process is sufficiently well developed—and Marx thought it already was in his day in Britain, Holland and the U.S.—it is possible (though not certain, and certainly not easy) for this transformation to occur through the ballot box. In any case, revolution takes up a whole period and generally involves many forms of struggle before the rules of the game that favor the existing ruling class are fully repealed.

It is also crucial to recognize that the main cause of revolutions is not revolutionaries but material conditions. The most important of these conditions are:

1) people's lives, which are already bad, are becoming worse;

2) a qualitatively better society has developed as a potential within the crevices of present-day society, and is recognized as a viable alternative by more and more people;

3) the oppressed are acquiring a unity that was previously lacking;

4) the failure to resolve worsening problems has led to a sharp drop in people's belief that existing social, political and economic arrangements are fair and/or can work;

5) fissures are opening up inside the ruling class, and between them and groups who until now have been faithfully serving them, principally the army, police, media, various kinds of professionals and the intelligentsia.

If, on top of all this, there are enough revolutionaries about to help people from the disadvantaged class(es) make the connections and draw the relevant political conclusions—the technical expression is "raising class consciousness"—a revolution can occur. What is called a "triggering incident," some new horror that brings the population to a boil against the regime, also plays an essential role, but such incidents are constantly occurring. They only become triggering, however, when the conditions I have just mentioned are present. Still, the full meaning of "revolution" will escape you until you can also make sense of the following: "Let me say, at the risk of seeming ridiculous, that the true revolutionary is guided by great feelings of love."—Che Guevarra

‡ Exam Psychology. How well you do on an exam will also be affected by how well you feel going in. A University of California study showed that listening to a little Mozart before an exam raised the test scores of many students. Why Mozart? Listen to some and find out. At the point of the exam, there is not much more you can do to relax than a little deep breathing. As for thinking positively, you might try concentrating on how well you did on some earlier exam, or the compliment you received for a piece of work you handed in, or on anything that makes you feel you can do it.

The relation between reform and revolution is clearly set out by the Polish Marxist, Rosa Luxemburg: "On the one hand, we have the day-to-day struggle; on the other, the social revolution. Such are the terms of the dialectical contradiction through which the socialist movement makes its way. It follows that this movement can best advance by tacking between the two dangers by which it is constantly being threatened, the loss of its mass character or the abandonment of its goal. One is the danger of sinking back to the condition of a sect; the other the danger of becoming a movement of bourgeois reform."

Every political party, of course, calls for "reforms." But, in our conservative era—as the writer Barbara Ehrenreich points out in the case of the Republican Party—this is a little like speaking of the Oklahoma City bombing as a "renovation." Real reforms involve changes that improve people's lives (always worth doing), while leaving the main problems of society untouched and the relations between classes as is. Every reform also has important contradictory effects on the class struggle. By demonstrating the flexibility of the ruling class and its supposed concern for the well being of ordinary people, reforms make the system appear more legitimate and hence more acceptable in the eyes of many. On the other hand, the struggle for reform, when successful—the ruling class seldom makes reforms on its own initiative—builds up the self-confidence of the oppressed and leaves them with the organizational and other means needed to intensify the struggle over other matters. Depending on which effect is dominant, a given reform may help to preempt a revolutionary upsurge or serve as a key part of it.

But with all the changes that have taken place in capitalism in its stage of globalization, the key question now is: Is capitalism still capable of being reformed? Despite the overwhelming evidence of recent failures, liberals and social democrats continue to answer "Yes." If you've come this far in the book, you know my answer.

‡ Exam Psychology. What about sex? Coaches often discourage their athletes from having sex the day before sporting events, because it takes too much of their energy and makes them too relaxed. If this were true—and I'm not sure it is—it might be a good reason for why super-charged people, who can't relax in other ways, should have sex the day before the exam. On the other hand, there is such a thing as coming into an exam too relaxed. To be handled gingerly.

TULI & ANON

Do we need a new party? Probably, but there already are over a dozen Left political parties and pre-party formations vying for your support. A mass party of workers (white collar as well as blue collar), led by workers, and serving working class interests (broadly understood) would be ideal, but we also need more organizations promoting socialist ideas at work, in schools and in communities, whether they call themselves parties or not.

Given the gross imbalance of forces at present, the main job now is to spread a socialist consciousness to people wherever they are and will listen. And, as life in capitalism continues to deteriorate and signs of a socialist alternative multiply and become increasingly hard to ignore, more and more people will be ready to listen. When "enough" people—and I don't know how many that is—understand that it is not Jews, or Blacks, or Japanese, or nature, or luck but *Capitalism* that is responsible for their worsening plight, questions of political strategy will appear in a new light and be much easier to answer. But don't wait until then to look for an answer, for your active search is an essential part of the process through which that answer will eventually emerge.

As part of your search, you might consider plastering the campus (town?) with copies of your favorite cartoons from this book, and, of course, inserting a few in all your letters and e-mails to friends, family, phone company (sure to be passed around by the workers), etc. Yeah, really.

‡ Exam Psychology. What about drugs? I have no personal experience with drugs, but, of course, I know some people who have used them. On the whole, this has usually led them to believe that they could do better on exams than they did. And there's the problem of side-effects and dependence. Better to do without.

What might the program of a revolutionary party look like? On the basis of the analysis offered in this book, here are a set of demands in the area of employment:

1) a choice of jobs for everyone who wants to work;
2) a chance to produce things that people actually need (i.e., want without having to be talked into them);
3) a living wage (which is easily double or triple the legal "minimum wage");
4) job security;
5) a safe, pleasant, ecologically sensitive job;
6) a chance to develop the skills needed to advance to a better job;
7) equality of opportunity and of treatment for everybody in the enterprise, whatever their race, gender, age, etc.;
8) democratic decision making, including the election of foremen and managers;
9) variety on the job and the chance to do two or more jobs in the place (and time) of one;

10) an opportunity to combine work and higher education or specialized training; and,

11) shorter and shorter hours of work, which is to say more free time to pursue other interests and develop other talents.

These are revolutionary demands because capitalism, however reformed, cannot satisfy them. Whereas, socialism can. As part of a program of a revolutionary party, they bring out what most workers want but build upon that to help workers imagine what they deserve. Taken together, these demands also point to the kind of structural changes that might be necessary for them to be satisfied. Our species not only deserves far more than capitalism now offers, but, given the rapidly deteriorating condition of our planetary home, we can no longer afford to settle for less.

‡ Exam Psychology. What about prayer? Anything that improves your self-confidence is a plus, so, if you think prayer works, go ahead. The same applies, of course, to bringing in a good luck charm or pouring salt over your shoulder. But remember the Christian saying that God helps those who help themselves, so don't depend too heavily on prayer, charms or salt.

Why socialism? All the arguments can be boiled down to the following:

1) if you are part of the working class—blue, white or pink collared—it's in your interests;

2) socialism is the only alternative to the material misery and other injustices associated with capitalism, and to the profit motivated destruction of the ecology that will soon render our planet unlivable;

3) developing cooperation and mutual concern is morally superior (on the basis of every major religious and non-religious system of morality) to promoting competition and mutual indifference;

4) organizing production and distribution to serve social needs on the basis of a democratically arrived at plan is more rational than allowing the vagaries of an uncontrolled market to determine both;

5) socialism is also more efficient, since unlike capitalism (especially in times of crisis), it would make full use of all the factors of production: machines/factories, raw materials and workers;
6) concerned with human values and beauty, it would bring the ugliness and shoddy character of most capitalist production to an end;
7) concerned with truth, it would make the false advertising, hype and outright lying that defiles so much of our public life unnecessary, and liberate knowledge so that it could serve all humanity rather than just the profit interests of a few;
8) concerned with equality, it would make the various oppressions that disfigure capitalism—of Blacks, women, etc.—dysfunctional of the economic order as well as illegal, and set about expunging the prejudice associated with them from people's minds; and,
9) concerned with freedom, for the first time in history, socialism would make everyone free to develop his/her full potential as a human being (which, not so incidentally, is Marx's definition of "freedom").

With so much going for socialism, the real question is why would anyone continue to support capitalism? Here, the best answer I've seen comes from a paper a student wrote for my course on "Socialist Thought": "I am not a socialist," she said, "because I like to own my own house, which in this case is bigger and nicer than my neighbor's. I am not a socialist because I want to inherit my father's fortune. I am not a socialist because I want to have the liberty of deciding to work or not...I am not a socialist because I prefer a Mercedes-Benz over a Datsun and a Cartier watch over a Timex. I do not blind myself by thinking that all have the same needs and interests, because we are all born different."

It makes sense ($ and cents) that this person opposes socialism. What is difficult to understand is why so many others—on whom this expensive shoe doesn't fit and never will—should agree with her.

‡ Are tests ineffective ways of finding out what you know? Usually. Do they give an unfair advantage to those who are comfortable because they have taken a lot of tests before? Without a doubt. Will they be corrected by someone with the usual amount of biases (meaning a lot) and a host of other quirks likely to affect your grade? Of course. Well, then, why exams, and especially why so many? The truth is that exams play less of a role in learning than in socializing and classifying students to suit the bureaucratic needs of our schools and the behavioral and ideological requirements of your future employers. They are essentially instruments of control and of learning how to be controlled. That's why tests are as much about your ability to take tests and directions as they are about knowledge. The role of education, as I've argued throughout this book, is minimal.

Yet, there is something else that gets tested here, something most examiners have not reckoned with, and that is "gamesmanship." If you understand what tests really are and how they work, you are in a position to be one up on your examiners. You can give them what they want and get a higher grade than you otherwise would, and through your success in manipulating exams reduce the degree to which they have manipulated and molded you. All readers of this book have been given what it takes to ring the bell on gamesmanship the next time they take an exam.

Okay, to be fair, I am now willing to admit that some of the better exams also test for what you know, but, though this is what gets everyone's attention, it is only worth a brief mention, and, then, only *after* its main social role has been clarified.

We don't have to accept this! There is a better way to run our society.

FIFTEEN

TEN COMMANDMENTS (COMMUNIST VERSION)

1) Thou shalt not put up with it any longer.

2) Thou shalt not believe them when they say that you have only yourself to blame for your plight.

3) Thou shalt not take your growing anger and frustration out on your loved ones or on your fellow sufferers.

4) Thou shalt not turn a blind eye to injustice, wherever you find it.

5) Thou shalt not leave those who have exploited your labor and the labor of your loved one in possession of their ill gotten gains.

6) Thou shalt not kill what's left of your life by failing to recognize that we can do better.

7) Thou shalt honor your father and mother, especially if they are trade union organizers or activists for other radical causes.

8) Thou shalt not covet your neighbor's good sense when she joins the socialist movement. (Do likewise.)

9) Thou shalt organize.

10) Thou shalt not fink out when the moment for action comes.

WOW!
ZING!
GREAT SHOOTING!
PING!
BOY- YOU'RE TERRIFIC!
WHAG!
LET'S SEE YOU HIT THAT HORNETS' NEST...
BZZZZZZZ
OH, NO! NOT THAT
NO? WHY NOT?
THEY'RE ORGANIZED!
OH!

‡ Readers shouldn't misunderstand my criticisms of exams in this book as opposition to a teacher asking questions. Questions are an essential part of education, but they should go in both directions. A give and take between students and teachers that includes a lot of questioning should be constant, even casual, but no less intense for all that. There is no need, however, to build up any of the questions coming from the teacher as the "Big Test," or to organize the discussion that precedes it as preparation for the test, or to grade the results. If some of you respond that absent such factors many students will not study at all, this only goes to show how far education in our society has become separated from genuine curiosity and felt needs. Who can deny that such alienation exists, and is even widespread?

The remedy lies in smaller, more intimate classes, student participation in drawing up the curriculum and course syllabi, and making it crystal clear from the start how what is taught is relevant to students' lives. And, of course, no one should be forced to take a course against his/her will. Required courses are the death knell of all serious learning. Most of these educational changes could only be carried out on the back of large scale social reform, but it is not too soon to begin thinking about what learning *should* be. It remains the case, that as far as real education is concerned—which means achieving a deep, permanent, critical and balanced understanding of the subject along with a desire to probe deeper into it—all the paraphernalia currently attached to question asking that transforms it into an *exam* are counterproductive.

Conservatives like to say that a person who is not a socialist at twenty has no heart, while someone who is still a socialist at forty has no head. Since the people who say this are usually older people who never were socialists, this could be a way of confessing that they never had a heart. I hope that the facts and arguments collected in this book show that they are also the ones without a head. With both heart and head calling for a socialist revolution, the only anatomical reason left for opposing socialism, it would appear—is cold feet.

Frederick Douglas, the Black freedom fighter and ex-slave, put it much better when he said, "If there is no struggle, there is no progress. Those who profess to favor freedom yet deprecate agitation are men who want crops without plowing the ground; they want the ocean without the awful roar of its many waters; they want rain without thunder and lightening. Power concedes nothing without demand. It never did and never will. Find out just what any people will quietly submit to and you have found out the exact measure of injustice and wrong that will be imposed upon them, and these will continue until they are resisted with either words or blows, or with both. The limits of tyrants are prescribed by the endurance of those they oppress."

‡ Finally, will Marxism help you do better on exams? I'd like to respond with an unambiguous "yes," but all I can offer is an ambiguous one. To the extent that it stresses change and interconnections, puts the university and the exam situation itself inside their proper social context, and makes you hip to who is really on your side and who isn't, Marxism should make you a more thoughtful person and a better student. To the extent, however, that it supplies you with a number of concepts—"class," "class struggle," "exploitation," "alienation," etc.— that your teachers themselves may not understand, and makes you impatient with the superficiality of most exams and angry at their all-too-frequent biases, Marxism could get you into trouble and result in lower grades. No matter how much good it does you, every strong medicine—and Marxism is one of the strongest—is capable of doing harm if used in the wrong way, or at the wrong time. So be careful, be wise—not furtive, but street-wise—and you may discover that the Marxism dispensed in this book helps you more with your exams than all my exam hints combined.

The place is Rome in the middle of the 5th century A.D.. The place is England in 1647. The place is France in 1788. The place is Russia in 1916. The place is Cuba in 1958. The place is the U.S. in (?). In none of these places and times did the majority of people think they were about to witness—and, in many cases, take part in—a major social and political revolution. They had, after all, never experienced such an event. And like people everywhere they probably believed that their future would always resemble their past. This generally results from putting too much weight on what people want or accept at any given moment. But conditions and people's reaction to them can change, and very quickly.

In 1962, for example, several sociologists led by John Goldthorpe conducted a major study of workers' attitudes at a Vauxhall automobile plant in Lutton, England. The workers were relatively well paid and the management more progressive than most. The conclusion, based on several hundred in depth interviews, was that overall the workers were pretty contented with their lot. Several months later, even before the book in which this study was written up reached the press, the same Vauxhall workers went on one of the most violent strikes in recent English history. No one, of course, was more surprised that the academics who had practically guaranteed that this would not happen. Also—just one more instance among many others—who expected the French working class to take over their enterprises nationwide in response to the repression of the student strikes that occurred in France in the Spring of 1968? Virtually no one, not the workers themselves, nor those who claimed to understand them.

So, don't despair on the basis of what is happening, or not happening, at this moment. A quiescent working class? The class struggle has gone into its seventh inning stretch, and those who know little about baseball and less about class struggle think the game is over. The decisive innings lie ahead. And history may yet deliver us a victory, especially if you...and you...and you stop acting against your own side in this struggle in the mistaken belief that in matters of this sort it's possible to be "a-political."

‡ What kind of exams do I give? In case you're wondering, apart from departmental graduate exams that I have to participate in, I haven't given an exam for over fifteen years. The truth is I don't believe that the work students do in preparing for an exam is the best way to acquire the kind of critical understanding I want them to have of the political theory and methodology courses that I teach. Nor do I believe that it is the best way of testing their knowledge; nor do I enjoy driving students' anxiety levels through the roof for a couple of weeks at the end of every term. In some courses, I require term papers, but for most I've requested students to keep an Ideas Notebook, a kind of intellectual diary, in which they both ask and answer questions raised by their readings, my lectures and events in the larger society. Students seem to enjoy doing the Notebooks, and appreciate having a record (which is returned to them) of how their thinking developed during the course.

"All power to the imagination"; "Be realistic, demand the impossible"; "Underneath the cobblestones [used in France for throwing at police] there is the beach"; "It is forbidden to forbid." These are some of the slogans of May, 1968, in France, which is about as close any developed capitalist country has come to having a socialist revolution. Marc Kravetz, now a leading French journalist, captures the unbridled enthusiasm of his fellow revolutionaries in these words: "Not all generations have a chance to live such a moment of freedom and joy. It was a huge collective fiesta."

Did I forget to mention it? Besides requiring hard work and dedication, revolutions are also enormously exciting and fun. Yes, *fun*, as even defenders of the status quo are forced to admit. Alain Robert, a member of the last conservative Government in France, recalls, "I was of course not on the side of the majority, but it was a very important movement. I'd like youths of today to be able to live a moment like that." (*International Herald Tribune*, June 1, 1993) I'd like youths of today to be able to live a moment like that as well, Alain.

‡ Cheating on exams. That's another book. I'll leave that one for the teacher who wants to tell you what a wonderful society capitalism is. Like all principles, however, this one too admits of an exception, and in this case it can be found in William H. Whyte's wonderful essay, "How to Cheat on a Personality Test," in his book, *The Organization Man*. No one should submit to an exam by a possible employer without reading it to learn just what will be held against you and why. This is one exam for which you have my blessings to cheat. For the others, even if you don't get caught, cheating is the loser's way out. Why bother, when you can win by learning how the game is played and playing it intelligently? To help you do this—in life as well as in exams—is what this book has been all about. Now—Go get them, Tiger! *Merde Puissance Treize!**

Bertolt Brecht wrote about a philosophy conference that was held to determine whether the Yellow River existed, which dragged on and on until the Yellow River overflowed and washed away the conference. Some, no doubt, will maintain that this was a terrible tragedy, because we still don't know whether the Yellow River exists. Others will see in this a warning not to tarry too long before doing what needs to be done.

* "Shit to the 13th power": The slang expression with which French students wish each other "good luck" before going in to take an exam.

Well, how is it going? I mean this book, and your experience reading it. And in case you are not yet ready to give me a review, let me write it for you (I've always wanted to review one of my own books, but until now I've lacked the *chutzbah* or, perhaps, the right book).

> "Ollman's *How To Take an Exam...and Remake the World* is driving me nuts, because I now see all the things I should have done in my last exam and didn't. How did I even pass? But thanks to all this good advice, I'll be ready, really ready, next time. Part of what makes me feel so sure is Ollman's account of what exams are all about other than education. No other self-help book in education does this double-duty work. Becoming savvy in how exams are used—not by teachers (they're just the hired hands)—to manipulate me into becoming the kind of docile worker and citizen required by those who run our society gives me the mental distance and the moral right to manipulate them back. I now know how to ace an exam without losing my soul in the process.
>
> Yet, while the mask of neutrality has been ripped away, the society-wide chains in which we are held remain. The other half of Ollman's book describes these chains, how and by whom they are applied, and what we can do to free ourselves. That, too, sets it apart from other self-help books in education. But, rather than Ollman taking on too much, maybe it's the other books that have taken on too little, taking the social game we are all forced to play for granted. What's the worth of an education that doesn't question the biased rules of this game, or of a self-help book in education that doesn't show us what we can do about it?"

Hey, now why didn't I say that?

I JUST FOUND OUT HOW THEY MAKE HAMBURGERS!
YOU LEFTISTS AND YOUR CONSPIRACY THEORIES. GET A GRIP ON YOURSELF, HONEY.

THE FUTURE

Choose Now—Pay Later

1. Socialism (all the objective conditions for building socialism are now in place).

2. Barbarism (the term is Marx's), a breakdown of civilization accompanied by endless civil wars (Somalia, Albania, Rwanda and Afghanistan probably give us the best indication of what barbarism would be like this time around).

3. A planet rendered uninhabitable by pollution or nuclear holocaust (at present rates of profit driven pollution, we have fifty to a hundred years to go—at most).

These are our *only* choices. As both everyday experience and Marx's analysis makes clear, democratic capitalism as it now exists cannot go on much longer. Hence, the most foolish "utopians" of all are the so-called "hard-headed realists," who assume that the present will continue into the indefinite future more or less unchanged. So, examine the alternatives *verrrry* carefully. Then *choose.* (Just keep in mind that either of the last two outcomes could also occur by default if you put off choosing too long.)

And to those readers who are wiggling frantically to get off the hook, I would only ask, "If not this, then what? If not you, then who? If not now, then when?" (With apologies to the *Talmud*)

END OF BOOK EXAM

I've managed to boil down the entire content of my course into one simple question: "How many capitalists does it take to screw in a light bulb?"

That's it. Really. You have ten seconds to answer. The correct answer and your grade can be found at the bottom of the next page.

THE LAST WORD

"Feelings"

Let us share joy and pain...

Let us dare everything...

What is to be avoided above all is

to say nothing,

And to want nothing, and to do nothing.

From a youthful poem by Karl Marx

or

In the words from a song by Victor Hara, Chilean poet and singer killed by General Pinochet: Remember, "Today is the time that could become tomorrow."

or

As Abbie Hoffman put it, "Leave a mark on history. There may not be money in it, but it's more exciting than studying accounting."

If you answered: "One (or more) to hire a worker to do it," you get a grade of 'F' and have to repeat the course—only no skipping pages this time. If you answered: "None," recognizing that we don't need capitalists to screw in light bulbs or do anything else that needs doing, you graduate with high honors, and can now go out and share what you've learned with others.

OLLMAN FAMILY PORTRAIT

Bertell, in a Reagan mask, and Paule, as a Contra devil, preparing for the Halloween Day Parade in New York City in 1985, where they protested against U.S. involvement in the Nicaraguan civil war.

‡ Life Exam Question: Who is the baby in the picture?

INDEX OF SUBJECTS, NAMES, CONCEPTS, IDEAS AND IMAGES

Now that you've kept your part of the bargain and read the whole book, here is an Index to help you use it to—what else?—take exams and remake the world.

CARTOONS AND PHOTOS:

Printed by the workers of
MARC VEILLEUX IMPRIMEUR INC.
Boucherville, Québec
for Black Rose Books Ltd.